Dining in HISTORIC OHIO

A Restaurant Guide With Recipes

by Marty Godbey

Illustrations by James Asher

McClanahan Publishing House

**Library of Congress Catalog Card Number: 87–060372
International Standard Book Number: 0–913383–08–2 $14.00**

Cover photograph: Bryn Mawr, Granville, Ohio
Courtesy Bryn Mawr

Illustrations by James Asher
Cover photograph by Don Pound Studio
Cover design by James Asher
Manufactured in the United States of America

All book order correspondence should be addressed to:
McClanahan Publishing House, Incorporated
Rt. 2 Box 32
Kuttawa, Kentucky 42055
(502) 388–9388

INTRODUCTION

The Ohio Country. Even the words must have sounded promising to New Englanders impoverished by the American Revolution. As soon as the area was reasonably safe from Indian attack, they flocked westward.

From Connecticut, pioneers ventured into the Western Reserve; those who had lost their homes to British depredation made new beginnings in the Firelands. Pennsylvanians floated down the Ohio River to found river towns, then moved inland, often in ethnic groups that formed the core of a hardworking, productive society.

After the War of 1812, soldiers who had fought in Ohio remembered the fertile valleys and plentiful water, and returned with their families. As immigration crowded the Eastern shores, newly-arrived Europeans headed west. Their craftsmanship began such needed industries as winemaking, brewing, tailoring, boatbuilding, mining, and ironmaking, and cities developed around these centers.

New England villages, German-speaking communities, and Virginia farms were established in Ohio, and flourished here, bringing a diversity that influenced both foods and architecture.

In less than a hundred years, Ohio changed from a sparsely populated and often dangerous frontier into one of the foremost industrial areas in the world. Despite rapid growth and change, buildings were carefully constructed, and thousands of nineteenth century structures remain in use.

Old taverns that once sheltered stagecoach travelers after a hard day's journey now serve tourists who cover that distance in less than an hour. Elegant homes, businesses, warehouses, factories, and mills have been adapted as restaurants, preserving their unique qualities and offering patrons a little history with their food.

Such unlikely structures as train stations, a covered bridge, a fire house, a winery, a pottery, and a hospital have been successfully converted to restaurants, giving new generations an opportunity to observe at first hand some of the places their ancestors took for granted.

"People are not only interested in a place to eat," said Gary Hewitt, whose pizza restaurants are housed in an 1862 covered bridge, "they want to be entertained by the place."

Surrounded by Shaker tools, railroad memorabilia, or art pottery, one is easily entertained by an old building, even before the food arrives. The personalities of those who built, lived, or worked in these structures lingers, and combines with those of the people who operate them to create very special places.

It would be easier and more economical to build a new restaurant with a spacious kitchen and labor-saving traffic patterns, but people who value the past realize you cannot create history, you can only appreciate it. When they utilize old buildings, despite the upkeep, space limitations, and inconvenience, they are giving something of themselves.

"A restaurant is not just a place to nourish the body, it's a place to nourish the soul," said Mary Louise Davis, who owns a converted Victorian mansion on a riverbank. "That's what Shield's Crossing is to a lot of people."

Although these buildings are old, their food reflects current interests; diners have acquired an enthusiasm for the new and different, as well as traditional favorites, and restaurants are eager to satisfy their tastes. Year-round supplies of fresh vegetables and seafoods have been important influences, as has an awareness of diet and nutrition in today's restaurant-goers.

A visit to any of Ohio's restaurants in historic buildings is well repaid, for an awareness of the past is as easily absorbed as the excellent food, and the diner leaves satisfied in more ways than one.

Using DINING IN HISTORIC OHIO
as a Travel Guide

A list of more than 200 restaurants in historic buildings in Ohio was accumulated from advertisements, history books, old travel guides, word-of-mouth reports, and personal experience. Each restaurant was investigated, and those selected for *Dining in Historic Ohio* were chosen on a basis of historic, architectural, and culinary interest, coupled with business stability.

So many good restaurants in Ohio occupy old buildings that only those which existed before 1900 were included, and the ultimate decision was made on preservation/restoration grounds. Of the 49 included, 30 are on the National Register of Historic Places.

Several early nineteenth-century taverns were disqualified because they had expanded over the years, obliterating all traces of original structures; other old buildings, in the hands of well-meaning but ignorant rehabilitators, had more recently lost their character. Those chosen all met the final criterion: they are places a first-time visitor would describe enthusiastically to friends.

The author, often with companions, ate anonymously in every restaurant on the original list at least once, ensuring the same treatment any hungry traveler might receive. No restaurant paid to be included; indeed, none knew of the project until asked to participate. They have been gracious and cooperative, some providing recipes that had never before been disclosed.

As an aid to travelers, the Ohio map has been divided into five sections; within each, restaurants are listed roughly from east to west. Resource information between text and recipes provides addresses and telephone numbers, and all travelers are encouraged to call before driving long distances.

Laws governing the sale of alcoholic beverages vary greatly. If beverages are available, it will be indicated in the resource information.

Symbols used for brevity include charge card references:

AE= American Express, CB= Carte Blanche, DC= Diner's Club, MC= Master Card, V= Visa.

Most of these restaurants would fall into the "moderate" category of expensiveness; an effort was made to include all price ranges, and special prices for children are indicated where offered. Using dinner entrée prices as a gauge, dollar signs are used to indicate reasonable ($), moderate ($$), and more expensive ($$$). Luncheon prices are usually significantly lower, and the amount of money spent in any restaurant is increased by the "extras" ordered, i.e., appetizers, drinks, and side orders.

Few of these restaurants would be considered expensive by East or West Coast standards; if cost is a determining factor, however, most restaurants will gladly provide a price range over the telephone.

Visitors are cautioned that although some of the restaurants in *Dining in Historic Ohio* are well off the beaten track, they may be very popular, and busy seasons are determined by local events that are often unfamiliar to non-residents. To avoid disappointment, **CALL AHEAD FOR RESERVATIONS.**

CONTENTS

I want to personally welcome you to the wonderful world of dining in Ohio.

Here, at the "heart of it all," you will find some of the most beautiful historic restaurants in the United States. Their cuisine represents not only the finest culinary traditions of our state, but also some of our most fascinating history.

In sheer variety of food products, Ohio serves more people than any single state in the nation. From the Great Lakes table fish to the ethnic and country foods throughout the state, our heartland cuisine offers a richness and diversity that delights both native Ohioans and visitors alike.

Ohio cuisine has been made famous by people whose ancestries cover all parts of the globe -- it is their great traditions that bring a fascinating variety and history to our great restaurants.

The pages of this book bring you a unique perspective on Ohio's past, as well as recipes that bring our heritage alive in your own kitchen.

Enjoy a living history as you travel through this book ... and through Ohio.

Best regards,

Richard F. Celeste

Richard F. Celeste
Governor

NORTH KINGSVILLE

UNIONVILLE

TOLEDO

MENTOR

ANDOVER

MAUMEE
PERRYSBURG
WATERVILLE

PORT CLINTON

CLEVELAND

BURTON
WELSHFIELD

GRAND RAPIDS

SANDUSKY

MILAN

BEREA

STRONGSVILLE

RICHFIELD

KENT

TIFFIN

CANTON

ELKTON

DELAWARE

COSHOCTON

WORTHINGTON
DUBLIN

GRANVILLE

LAFAYETTE

COLUMBUS

MIAMISBURG

GERMANTOWN

MARIETTA

LEBANON

GLENDALE

LOVELAND
MILFORD

CHILLICOTHE

CINCINNATI

IRONTON

OHIO

0   20   40   60

Miles

THE LEVEE HOUSE CAFÉ
Marietta

On March 1, 1786, eleven men met at The Bunch of Grapes Tavern in Boston to form The Ohio Company of Associates. Some were veterans of the American Revolution, who wished to use their army pay to purchase land— Continental currency was worthless for other purposes, being valued at about twelve cents on the dollar.

The Land Ordinance of 1787 established that lands in The Northwest Territory would eventually come into the Union as equal states. In this new area, there would be religious freedom and the right of trial by jury, slavery would be prohibited, and education encouraged.

The Ohio Company bought 1,500,000 acres in what is now southeastern Ohio, and forty-seven men under General Rufus Putnam landed at the confluence of the Ohio and Muskingum Rivers on April 7, 1788, to found Ohio's first settlement.

The new town of Marietta prospered, becoming a cultural center with business based on river transportation. Much of historic interest has been preserved, and the entire downtown was placed on the National Register of Historic Places in 1974. Each year, the weekend after Labor Day, thousands attend Marietta's Sternwheel Festival on the Ohio River.

One original riverfront structure remains, a drygoods store built about 1826 for Dudley Woodbridge, first merchant in the Northwest Territory. The narrow three-story Federal style brick building served for a time as a waterfront hotel, and its one-story addition, built in 1911 as a saloon, was later used for car repairs.

Condemned by the 1980s, the shell of the building was rebuilt by preservationist Harley Noland with parts of local buildings: a pressed-tin ceiling from a clothing store destroyed by fire, marble from a demolished bank, and gas light fixtures stored since electricity came to town.

With co-owners Bill Greenlees and Chef Ellen Morgenthaler, he opened The Levee House Café in 1983. Tall windows in the crisp white dining room overlook the Ohio River, and bright blue furniture from a 1940s tavern adds a cheery note. The former saloon/garage became another dining room in Spring, 1987, proving the popularity of Chef Ellen's innovative cooking.

She describes Levee House food as "All the real thing, fresh foods, everything made from scratch except sandwich breads." A summer lunch under the awning might include potato-cheese soup; a salad of new potatoes, celery, and green onion in vinaigrette; or an open-faced Italian Melt of salami, marinated vegetables, melted mozzarella and sprouts.

Dinner menus reflect the freshest meats and vegetables cleverly prepared— Blue Cheese Chicken is a favorite— and both meals feature Pastry Chef Gayle Shank's outrageous desserts. Try the Sour Cherry Chocolate Torte, dense and pudding-y; Banana Nut Cake with cream cheese frosting; or flaky old-fashioned pies with a blob of whipped cream. You can't go wrong here!

The Levee House Cafe, 127 Ohio Street, Marietta, Ohio 45750, is open 11:30 a.m. to 2:30 p.m., and 5:30 to 9:30 p.m., Tuesday through Saturday, and 10:30 a.m. to 1:30 p.m. for Sunday Brunch. (614)374-2233. There is no dress code, wine and beer are served (except Sunday), and reservations are suggested, especially for outside tables in Summer. MC, V, Discover. ($$)

LEVEE HOUSE CAFÉ BLACK BEAN SOUP

1 or 1 ½ pounds black
  beans
2 large onions
3 or 4 carrots
6 cloves garlic
4 celery stalks with leaves
3 or 4 Tablespoons oil
1 Tablespoon ground
  coriander
1 Tablespoon ground
  cumin

1 cup orange juice
½ cup sherry wine
2 oranges, peeled, seeded,
  and chopped
1 teaspoon ground black
  pepper
½ teaspoon cayenne
  pepper

Soak beans overnight. Drain, rinse, and place in large pot. Cover with 1 gallon water and cook over medium heat. Chop onions, garlic, and celery, and saute in oil until onion is translucent; add to beans. Add remaining ingredients and cook, stirring occasionally, until beans are tender. Serves 12.

LEVEE HOUSE CAFÉ CHICKEN-CUCUMBER SALAD

5 cups cooked, cubed
  chicken
2 cups peeled, seeded,
  diced cucumber
½ cup thinly sliced celery
  with tops

¼ cup diced canned
  pimiento
1 Tablespoon dill weed
2 or 3 Tablespoons white
  vinegar
Mayonnaise

Toss all ingredients except mayonnaise; let stand 15 or 20 minutes. Add enough mayonnaise to moisten and mix well. Serve on lettuce leaves, garnished with fresh fruit or vegetables or black olives or quartered hard-boiled egg. Serves 6.

LEVEE HOUSE CAFÉ SOUR CREAM APPLE PIE

One 10-inch unbaked pie
  shell
1 ½ cups sour cream
1 cup sugar
⅓ cup flour
Dash of salt

2 eggs
3 cups peeled, cored, sliced
  apples
1 ½ teaspoons vanilla
¾ teaspoon cinnamon
Crumb topping (see below)

Combine sour cream with other ingredients, pour into pie shell and bake at 400 degrees for 30 minutes. Sprinkle with topping, return to oven and bake an additional 20 to 30 minutes.

For crumb topping: Cut 7 Tablespoons butter into 1 cup flour and ⅓ cup sugar until crumbly.

Variations: use first four ingredients, with one egg, 3 cups fresh blueberries, juice and grated zest of one lemon, ½ teaspoon nutmeg. Or substitute 3 cups sliced fresh peaches or 3 cups fresh or well-drained canned, water-pack sour cherries.

THE SHADYBROOK INN
Ironton

A large outcropping of sandstone gave its name to a town in southeastern Ohio called "Hanging Rock." Iron ore was discovered nearby, and by 1849, there were seventeen "hot blast' and five "cold blast" furnaces in operation in an area known as the Hanging Rock Iron Region.

John Campbell, an ironmaster from Ripley, and a pioneer in the hot blast method, founded a town he called "Ironton" near Hanging Rock about 1848. Iron was shipped on the Ohio River, but after railroads opened up inland areas, Ironton became a boom town. Each furnace was named, and Ironton was the home of "Big Etna," the largest blast furnace in the world, and "Hecla," the furnace which cast wheels for early railroads.

By 1880, ore was giving out. Purer ore from the Lake Superior region could be shipped to Cleveland and Youngstown, which were close to coal-mining districts, and iron and steel mills moved north. Ironton adapted to the changes, however, and continues to be the industrial center of the tri-state area.

About 1890, a two-story frame house in the Queen Anne style was built in Ironton by a prosperous family named Bull. It passed through Cook and Davis families before being converted to a restaurant, "The Shadybrook Inn," named for a popular restaurant and lake which were lost when U.S. 52 was widened.

Well-lighted dining rooms downstairs feature original stained-glass and oak woodwork; doorways were skillfully widened to conform to access regulations, and original doors now panel one dining room. The friendly feeling of a gracious home is evident at The Shadybrook Inn under the supervision of manager Larry Chinn.

Larry, an Ironton native who spent ten years opening new restaurants for a national chain, appreciates the neighborliness of The Shadybrook Inn. "It's more of a home atmosphere," he said. "We basically have all home people here; there are no outside influences— it's home owned and operated."

That may help account for the down-home flavor of the food. There's a different homemade soup for lunch every day, with lots of sandwiches on your choice of bun, whole wheat or rye bread or a croissant; burgers any way you like them, and the Shadybroiler: turkey, bacon, and tomato, smothered in Cheddar cheese and broiled.

Dinner selections include prime rib, broiled fish, steaks, fried shrimp and oysters, and terrific sautéed chicken livers, plus specials— usually four different chicken items every night.

Vegetable accompaniments, salads, and hot breads are a taste of real country food, but desserts are unforgettable: warm apple dumpling in a soft, buttery crust, with cinnamon hearts and ice cream, strawberry shortcake on a real biscuit short-cake, and five to eight different homemade pies every day, all of them excellent.

The Shadybrook Inn, 803 Vernon Street, Ironton, Ohio 45638, is on the corner of 8th Street, one block off the downtown Ironton exit from U.S. 52. It is open Monday through Saturday; lunch is 11 a.m. to 2 p.m., and dinner is 5 to 10 p.m. "Early Eaters" from 4 to 6 p.m. have a special menu at reduced prices. (614)532-6491. Dress is casual, all legal beverages are available, and reservations are requested, and necessary for parties of ten or more. AE. MC, V. ($$)

SHADYBROOK INN BAKED CORN

48 ounces fresh OR frozen
  corn
1 egg
½ cup milk
2 Tablespoons vanilla
2 Tablespoons + 2
  teaspoons melted butter

⅔ cup sugar
⅔ cup flour
2 teaspoons baking soda
Cinnamon

Spread corn in buttered 9″ x 13″ pan or baking dish. In large mixing bowl, place liquid ingredients; add dry ingredients, blend well, pour over corn and sprinkle with cinnamon. Bake at 350 degrees about one hour, or until done. Serves 10.

SHADYBROOK INN CABBAGE AND ONIONS

Shredded cabbage
Chopped onions
Powdered garlic

Salt
Vegetable oil

In skillet, sauté cabbage and onions, seasoned to taste, in vegetable oil, until onions are white and clear, and cabbage is tender. Drain off oil before serving.

SHADYBROOK INN SWEET AND SOUR BAKED CHICKEN

One 3-pound chicken
1 teaspoon salt
2 Tablespoons vinegar
2 Tablespoons prepared
   mustard

2 Tablespoons brown
   sugar

Season chicken with salt. Combine vinegar with mustard and brown sugar. Place long sheet of foil in baking dish large enough to hold chicken. Place chicken on foil, brush with vinegar mixture, and seal foil around chicken. Bake at 350 degrees for about an hour and a half, or until chicken is done.

SHADYBROOK INN FRENCH CHOCOLATE SILK PIE

One 9-inch baked pie shell
   OR Graham cracker
   crust
2 ounces unsweetened
   chocolate OR 6
   Tablespoons cocoa + 1
   Tablespoon butter or
   margarine

½ cup butter or margarine
¾ cup sugar
1 teaspoon vanilla
3 eggs
Whipped cream for
   garnish
Toasted pecans or
   almonds

In small saucepan, melt chocolate. In mixer bowl, cream butter with sugar, add chocolate and vanilla. Blend thoroughly. Add eggs, one at a time, beating five minutes after each. Pour mixture into prepared shell and refrigerate. Garnish with whipped cream and toasted nuts. Serves 8.

THE HARVESTER
Chillicothe

The Indian name "Chalah-gawtha," meaning "place,' was given to several Indian encampments. Colonel Nathaniel Massie, claiming his lands in the Virginia Military District, laid out a town at the mouth of Paint Creek in 1796; it was near an earlier Indian village, and he named it "Chillicothe.'

By 1803, there were seventy cabins and a dozen frame houses in the village, and Edward Tiffin, Chillicothe resident and statehood advocate, was named the first governor of Ohio. Chillicothe became the first capital, and the State Seal was inspired by a sunrise behind Mount Logan, just outside town.

Even after the capital was permanently located in Columbus in 1816, Chillicothe continued to grow. The trading and processing center of a prosperous farming community, it became an industrial town as well, specializing in the manufacture of paper.

A red brick commercial building called "Carlisle Corner" was built at Main and Paint streets in 1885. The four-story Second Empire structure sported a rounded corner tower, and housed a department store, a drugstore, numerous shops, and offices on the upper floors. With the Chillicothe Business District, it was placed on the National Register in 1979.

In 1974, the former department store became a restaurant with balcony seating overlooking an airy, open dining room, and a tavern in its stone-walled cellar. In 1980, it was bought by Cathy Bryer, who is certified to teach food service in vocational schools, and has applied these skills in her restaurant. "Our goal is to give the customer the best service in the most comfortable atmosphere with the least amount of interruption," she said. "And the best food, too."

Customers appreciate "Homemade lunch" at the Harvester, that might feature meatloaf, Salisbury steak, or pork chop and kraut. There are burgers and sandwiches, "fix your own" salads, and light entrées of chicken, beef, or quiche.

Dinner items are heartier, more modern, with specials devised from fresh seafoods or new recipes, plus a lengthy menu of ribs, steaks, seafoods, and chicken. All include salad, potato, and hot homemade bread with apple butter.

Soups— an outstanding cream of broccoli— and desserts

23

at any meal are exciting. Country pies and ice cream croissants are joined by a rich oatmeal cake with broiled coconut topping. A customer was overheard saying, "This Harvester Cake is the best thing I ever tasted!" You may agree.

The Harvester Restaurant, 9 South Paint Street, Chillicothe, Ohio 45601, is open for lunch 11 a.m. to 3 p.m. Monday through Friday, for dinner 5 to 10 p.m. Monday through Thursday, until 11 Friday and Saturday, plus extended hours with food service in "The Cellar." (614)773-4663. Dress is casual, all legal beverages are served, with premium wines by the glass and many bottled wines from the adjacent wine shop. Reservations are accepted, and children's and seniors' portions of some entrees are available. AE, DC, MC, V. ($$$)

HARVESTER SWISS ONION SOUP

1 stick butter OR
  margarine
2 large onions, chopped
2 ounces beef base*
2 ounces chicken base*
2 quarts hot water

¼ cup dry sherry wine
1 quart cold water
2 cups flour
Seasoned croutons
Slices of Swiss cheese

In soup pot, melt butter, add onions, and saute until tender, but not brown. Dissolve beef and chicken bases in hot water, add to onions, add sherry, and bring to boil. Thoroughly mix flour with cold water; add very slowly to boiling soup, whipping vigorously. After all is added, reduce to a simmer, stirring often. To serve, top each crock of soup with croutons and a slice of cheese. Melt under broiler. About 10 servings.

* Meat bases are commercial preparations not readily available to the consumer. Substitute 1 quart chicken stock and 1 quart beef stock for the meat bases and 2 quarts hot water.

HARVESTER HAM LOAF

1 pound ham, ground
1 pound fresh pork,
  ground
2 eggs
1 ¼ cups milk

⅔ cup crushed saltine
  crackers
⅓ cup tapioca
Dressing (see below)

In large bowl, mix all ingredients. Form into a loaf and pour dressing over. Let stand a few minutes until it soaks into loaf. Bake at 350 degrees about 1 ½ hours.

For dressing: Boil together ¼ cup vinegar, ½ cup water, ⅓ cup brown sugar, and 1 Tablespoon prepared mustard.

HARVESTER CAKE

1 ½ cups brown sugar
1 ½ cups sugar
3 eggs
1 ½ sticks butter, melted
3 teaspoons cinnamon
1 ½ teaspoons baking soda
¾ teaspoon salt
¾ teaspoon baking powder
2 ¼ cups flour
1 ½ cups quick oats, cooked in 2 cups boiling water

In large bowl, mix all ingredients in order given. Pour into greased 9″ x 13″ pan, and bake at 350 degrees about 40 minutes, or until firm. Do not overbake. While still warm, spread with topping (see below) and BROIL until bubbly and brown. Cut into squares to serve 12.

For topping, blend:
1 ½ cups brown sugar
3 cups grated coconut
1 ½ sticks butter, melted
1 ½ teaspoons vanilla
6 ounces evaporated milk

COVERED BRIDGE PIZZA
North Kingsville

Coffee grinders, butter churns, and covered bridges— as soon as a tool passes from daily use, it becomes a focus for nostalgia. People collect the smaller items, and drive for miles to observe and photograph larger ones, before they disappear entirely.

There are twelve historic covered bridges in Ashtabula County, plus two new ones; they are frequently visited and photographed, and are even honored by an annual festival the second weekend in October, but they are not likely to

COVERED BRIDGE PIZZA
Andover

dissappear. Indeed, if fund-raising efforts go well, a third new bridge will follow shortly, in a county that calls itself "Covered Bridge Capital of the Western Reserve."

The first covered bridge in America crossed the Schuylkill River at Philadelphia in 1805. Wood was an ideal construction material, readily available on site, easily worked, and durable if protected. Roofs, contrary to popular opinion, were not built to shelter lovers, but to protect the wooden structures from weather.

By mid-nineteenth century, there were more than 40 covered bridges in Ashtabula County. Typically, they were built on stone pilasters, with strong beams spanning the stream, crossed by heavy joists and layers of flooring. Their height above the streams was important; ice and rising waters in the spring were a hazard.

As new roads and modern bridges were built, few covered bridges were left; in 1942, there were only twenty-seven. When the Forman Road Bridge in Eagleville was washing out in 1972, the county advertised it for sale. A sealed bid of $5.00— the only bid— was made by Gary Hewitt, who was given sixty days to take it down.

The bridge, built in 1862, was 126 feet long, and weighed 55 tons. "All the pieces were numbered, and pictures were taken," said Hewitt, who stored the pieces for three years, awaiting permits to reconstruct the bridge as a restaurant. "When we got approval," he said, "we got out the pictures and put it together like a puzzle. It was kind of fun."

Hewitt used half the bridge for a pizza restaurant in North Kingsville in 1975, and the other half for a similar restaurant in Andover in 1977. In both cases, the interior utilized only original materials, insulated and protected by new siding and new roofs outside.

The two resulting bridges are positioned to give a realistic appearance, and the interiors have the dim, mysterious charm of a functioning covered bridge. Wooden booths and tavern-style tables are comfortable beneath the original roof trusses, lit by light fixtures with yellow globes. The 4" x 8" supporting posts are held together by huge wooden pegs in a lattice-like pattern, through which the original exterior walls are visible, complete with carvings.

"So many people who lived around that area come to look for initials they put there as kids, and talk about how they used to fish off that bridge," Hewitt said. "We have people who drive thirty or forty miles to buy pizza here and see the old bridge."

It's worth the drive for the pizza, too.

Extraordinarily good, it is available in white or whole wheat, thin or regular crust, with cheese and all toppings generously distributed. Crusts are homemade daily, tomato sauce is rich, without being sweet, and there is also a garlic or "white pizza," without sauce, just cheeses and spices, and your choice of toppings.

Other offerings include salads, homemade chili and soup of the day, spaghetti with meatballs or meat sauce, all served with miniature loaves of homemade bread. There is every kind of submarine sandwich, or you can create your own combination.

At the North Kingsbridge location, you can even have a pizza for dessert, a crunchy shortbread crust, spread with cream cheese, topped with fruit, and sprinkled with coconut. It looks like a pizza, is served in wedges like a pizza, but tastes— well, like pizza DESSERT. You'll love it!

Covered Bridge Pizza, 6541 S. Main Street, North Kingsville, Ohio, (216)224-0497 or 224-2252, and 380 E. Main Street, Andover, Ohio, (216)293-6776. Mailing address for both is P.O. Box 267, North Kingsville, Ohio 44068. Hours are the same in both locations: Monday through Thursday, and Sunday, 11 a.m. to 12 midnight, Friday and Saturday 11 a.m. to 1 a.m., with continuous service. No alcoholic beverages are served, and dress is casual. Monday and Tuesday are family nights, with reduced prices. Guests are provided with a map and history of other covered bridges in the county. No charge cards are accepted. ($)

COVERED BRIDGE PIZZA DESSERT

1 cup sugar	¼ cup sugar
1 cup margarine	One 21-ounce can cherry
1 egg	pie filling
2 ½ cups flour	One 17-ounce can fruit
1 teaspoon baking soda	cocktail, drained
Pinch of salt	Shredded coconut
8 ounces cream cheese	Chopped nuts

Mix first six ingredients and pat on greased 14-inch pizza pan. Bake at 350 degrees for 15 minutes, or until light brown.

Blend cream cheese with sugar and spread on baked shortbread. Mix fruit and spread on cheese mixture, sprinkle with coconut and chopped nuts. Cool; cut into wedges to serve.

29

LOCK 24
Elkton

The routes of the Ohio and Erie Canal, from Cleveland to Portsmouth, and the Miami and Erie, from Toledo to Cincinnati, were determined after hot debate, and other canals were proposed to link with them.

One of the smaller canals, privately financed, was named for the two streams it followed across east-central Ohio: Little Beaver Creek, which flowed into the Ohio, and Sandy Creek, a tributary of the Tuscarawas.

Ground was broken for The Sandy and Beaver Canal in 1834, and by 1836, there were 2,000 men at work. High ground along the canal required two tunnels— one 3,180 feet long— which were hand drilled and blasted through solid stone. Work was slow. Although eastern and western sections were in use by the late 1830s, the summit division, requiring a "climb" of 164 feet, was not open until 1848.

It was used for only four years; railroads destroyed its usefulness, and investors lost heavily, selling portions of the canal to whomever would buy.

At Lock 24 on the Sandy and Beaver, near Elkton, an 1830s barn has been converted to an unusual restaurant and several gift shops. The lower level, which once housed cattle, is now a rustic dining room, with a greenhouse addition that overlooks the lock and the smallest covered bridge in the United States.

The restaurant, opened in 1977, is owned and operated by two generations of one family: Paul and Arlene Pugh, son Jim and his wife Ely, and daughter Marilyn Pasco. "My mother is famous for her carrot muffins," Jim said, "and my wife is the brain and idea person in the kitchen."

The combination is unbeatable. Hot breads passed before meals are crusty and flavorful, and Ely's French training shows in her skillful combinations of ingredients. At lunch, soups by cup or crock are followed by omelets, sandwiches— Baltimore Crab Cake Sandwich is not the only remarkable one— and salads such as "The Ultimate," with asparagus, hearts of palm, watercress, cucumbers, and ripe olives.

Dinner menus should carry a warning: vegetable haters will change their minds. Choices are many, fresh and delectable, and sometimes hard to identify. Who'd think of orange-flavored acorn squash squares with breadcrumbs, scalloped potato quiche, or julienne jicama with snow peas? They're deftly chosen to enhance such entrées as chicken and apricots in lime cream, shrimp Dijon, and beef tenderloin with Roquefort and Parmesan cheeses. "Wild Month" each November provides a chance to eat game in a variety of preparations.

There is always a featured wine, and "Exotique Cafés" from the espresso, as well as "Sinful" desserts. Poached pear with custard-rum AND double chocolate fudge sauces, Midnight Layer Cake, and pecan pie with butter-cookie crust are just a few.

Lock 24, P.O. Box 24, Elkton, Ohio 44415, is one mile east of Ohio 11 on Ohio 154, and is open Tuesday through Friday with continuous service. Lunch is 11 a.m. to 3 p.m., "Early dining' (at reduced prices) is 3 to 6 p.m., and dinner 5 to 10 p.m. Saturday lunch is 11:30 a.m. to 3 p.m., and dinner is 5 to 10 p.m. (216)424-3710. All legal beverages are served, dress is casual, and reservations are preferred for dinner, and for parties of more than six. AE, MC, V. ($$$)

LOCK 24 STUFFED MUSHROOMS WITH WALNUTS AND CHEESES

8 to 10 jumbo mushrooms
3 Tablespoons butter
3 Tablespoons onion, finely chopped
1 clove garlic, crushed
1 teaspoon chopped parsley
⅓ cup chopped walnuts
Salt and pepper
½ cup grated Swiss cheese
¼ cup grated Parmesan cheese
Juice of one lemon, divided
Bread crumbs
8 to 10 ounces frozen spinach, thawed
3 Tablespoons vegetable oil

Break stems from mushrooms, chop, measure ½ cup, and set aside. In saucepan, heat butter; saute onion and garlic until tender. Add stems, parsley, walnuts, salt and pepper, and stir. Cook five minutes; remove from heat. Mix in cheeses, 1 teaspoon lemon juice, bread crumbs, and spinach that has been squeezed dry. Toss mushroom caps in remaining lemon juice and oil. Stuff with cooled filling and roll additional in bread crumbs. They will hold several hours. Bake at 400 degrees for 10 to 15 minutes, and serve hot.

LOCK 24 SWEET AND WHITE POTATO DAUPHINOISE

2 medium baking potatoes
2 medium sweet potatoes
3 Tablespoons butter

1 clove garlic, crushed
Salt and pepper
1 cup heavy cream

Parboil potatoes about 20 minutes. Drain, slice thin, and set aside. Butter 2-quart casserole, rub with garlic, and layer potatoes, alternating white and sweet. Season between layers; pour cream over. Bake at 350 degrees until golden brown.

LOCK 24 SAUTÉED SPAGHETTI SQUASH

1 medium spaghetti
   squash
3 Tablespoons butter
½ green pepper, diced
½ red pepper, diced
1 small zucchini, diced

1 yellow squash, diced
Salt and pepper
1 tomato, diced
Grated Parmesan and
   Swiss cheese for topping

In shallow pan with ½-inch water, bake spaghetti squash in 350 degree oven about 35 minutes, or until you can pierce with a fork. Cool. Cut in half, scoop out seeds, then fold pulp out of shell and set aside. Melt butter in skillet, and saute peppers, zucchini, and yellow squash. Season, add spaghetti squash and tomato, and heat through. Arrange on serving plate and top with cheeses.

THE OLD TAVERN
Unionville

In her original land grant from King Charles II of England in 1662, Connecticut was given a patent on lands west to the "South Sea" or Pacific Ocean. Claims of other eastern states were just as general, frequently overlapping, and those who purchased or were granted land were often involved in title disputes— maps were inaccurate and records were poorly kept.

The U.S. Congress, during and immediately after the Revolution, persuaded the states to cede their rights to western lands "to be disposed of for the common benefit of the United States.' Disputes would thus be settled, and revenue from the sale of these lands would aid the impoverished young country. As soon as population growth warranted, new states would be formed and admitted to the Union.

Certain areas were retained by the states. Virginia kept the Virginia Military District, in the southwestern part of Ohio, and Connecticut, having already given up land to Pennsylvania, reserved 3,000,000 acres in what is now northeastern Ohio. Portions of this land were granted to Revolutionary soldiers in payment for their services; in the Western Reserve, land sales benefited Connecticut's schools.

Soon after the Greeneville treaty of 1795 promised safety from Indian attack, settlers began flocking westward from New England along the Buffalo-Cleveland route. A log tavern believed to have been built in 1798 became such a popular stop that it was greatly enlarged.

By the early 1800s, when the population of the Western Reserve was 1,300 people, it was a dignified three-story clapboard saltbox, with a large common-room, cozy dining rooms and a second-story ballroom that made it a center for local entertainment as well as for travelers. When huge whitewood posts and a classical portico were added about 1820, the tavern achieved the appearance it still has.

Over the years, it was called Webster House, New England House, and Union House, and, except that overnight business has ended, is much the same as The Old Tavern. It was placed on the National Register in 1973.

"We don't want to make any changes," said Ralph Haskins, who, with his son Gary, purchased the tavern in the summer of 1986. "It's been here 188 years, and we think it'll last another five years."

Visitors may eat in the original log cabin room, before the fire in the blue room, or in the yellow verandah, overlooking an enclosed garden. All rooms are filled with antiques and artifacts that reflect the tavern's colorful past.

Justly famed for homemade pies and round corn fritters in a pool of maple syrup, The Old Tavern's food follows country tradition. Luncheons of fried chicken, baked ham, and round of beef include potatoes, salad, fritter, and dessert; also available are salads, sandwiches, and light fare. Popular dinners are roast duck, rack of lamb, seafoods and steaks, served with potato, salad, fritter, relish, and hot breads.

If available, don't miss the "open top" fresh raspberry pie or rhubarb pie made of home grown, home-canned rhubarb.

The Old Tavern, 7935 S. Ridge Road, Unionville, Ohio 44088, is on Ohio 84, off I-90 at Geneva or Madison. It is open for lunch 11 a.m. to 2:30 p.m. and dinner 5 to 9 p.m., Monday through Saturday, and on Sunday from 12 Noon to 7 p.m., with continuous service. (216)428-2091. Dress is casual, and all legal beverages are served, including Sunday. Reservations are suggested, and are a necessity on Sunday. AE, DC, MC, V. ($$)

THE OLD TAVERN THOUSAND ISLAND DRESSING

2 cups mayonnaise or
  salad dressing
½ cup chili sauce
1 ½ hard-cooked eggs
½ cup pickle relish

¼ cup powdered sugar
¾ teaspoon salt
1 ½ teaspoons grated
  onion

Mix all ingredients, and store in refrigerator in covered jar. Yields about 3 cups.

THE OLD TAVERN OATMEAL MUFFINS

2 cups oatmeal
1 cup (packed) brown
  sugar
½ cup seedless raisins
2 eggs
2 Tablespoons melted
  margarine

2 cups buttermilk
1 ⅞ cups sifted flour
2 teaspoons baking
  powder
1 teaspoon baking soda
½ teaspoon salt

In large bowl, place oatmeal, brown sugar, and raisins. Beat together eggs, margarine, and buttermilk, and add to oatmeal mixture. Sift together remaining ingredients and add. Fill greased muffin tins half full and bake at 300 degrees for 15 minutes, or until golden brown. Makes 2 dozen+ large muffins.

THE OLD TAVERN PECAN PIE

One 9-inch pastry shell
½ cup sugar
1 cup dark corn syrup
¼ teaspoon salt
1 Tablespoon flour

2 eggs
1 Tablespoon melted
  butter
1 teaspoon vanilla
1 ¼ cups pecan meats

In large bowl, beat together all ingredients but pecans. Stir in pecans and pour into pastry shell. Bake at 300 degrees for one hour or until just set. If a brown crust is desired, brush edges with evaporated milk before baking. Serves 8.

BURTON FOX INN
Burton

The hardy souls from Cheshire, Connecticut, who settled Geauga County, came in small bands, or by families, to carve homes out of the wilderness. They were farmers who also produced cheese and quantities of syrup from the plentiful maple trees, but they were dependent upon the weather, which was often harsh.

In the little community of Burton, five acres that had belonged to town founder Eleazer Hickox was transferred in 1832 to James Peffers, the village postmaster.

The small frame house he lived in served also as Post Office, and remained in the Peffers family until 1975, being repeatedly enlarged, and becoming an inn in 1925.

The present owner, restaurateur Charles Imars, utilized portions of two old barns to add a rear wing, and opened The Burton Fox Inn in the summer of 1986.

Despite additions and changes, there is a pleasant feeling of age in this cozy house, and the service makes guests feel welcome. Homemade hot breads— popovers, blueberry muffins, and sticky buns— are instantly presented with butter and homemade raspberry jam just the color of the dining room walls. All before you even order.

"We're serving what we consider to be highly standardized Colonial food of different regions," Imars said, "influenced by people who came from other countries and by what was available in our country.'

Chef John Iacofano doesn't take shortcuts, and everything is prepared from scratch, including bakery items, salad dressings, and ice creams.

Lunch might be one of the three soups made daily— the chili is rich and delicious— and a Monte Cristo sandwich with Geauga County maple syrup, or a traditional Welsh Rarebit over toast points. Salads include eighteenth century Salmagundi with ham, turkey, cheese, and tomato, and Chesapeake Bay salad with crabmeat.

Dinner choices are many, from Sherried Chicken Breast to Tidewater Oyster and Lobster Pye, or venison chops with mushrooms. Numerous vegetable and potato accompaniments (don't miss the corn fritter drenched in maple syrup) are always interesting. And desserts are what you'd like to think

George Washington feasted on: baked custard with caramel sauce, meringue with homemade ice cream and Melba sauce, and a dense, chocolate-y "Red Devil" cake with custard filling and rich chocolate frosting.

The Burton Fox Inn, 14656 South Cheshire Street, Burton, Ohio 44021, is open for lunch 11:30 a.m. to 3 p.m., Monday through Saturday, for dinner 5:30 to 9 p.m. Monday through Thursday, until 11 p.m. Friday and Saturday. "Morsels" are available between 3 and 5:30. Sunday Buffet Brunch is 10:30 a.m. to 2 p.m., and dinner from 2 to 7 p.m. (216)729-3663. Dress is casual, all legal beverages are served, including Sunday, and reservations are accepted EXCEPT Saturday from 7:30 to 9 p.m. Children's menu is available. MC, V. ($$$)

BURTON FOX INN PHILADELPHIA STICKY BUNS

1 package yeast
¼ cup warm water
1 cup milk, scalded
4 ½ cups flour, divided
½ cup + 2 Tablespoons
    melted butter, divided
6 Tablespoons sugar,
    divided

2 egg yolks, beaten
1 teaspoon salt
Grated rind of 1 lemon
1 teaspoon cinnamon
½ cup currants
¾ cup brown sugar

Sprinkle yeast over water and dissolve. Combine with cooled milk and 1 ½ cups flour and beat well. Let rise. Add 4 Tablespoons butter, 4 Tablespoons sugar, yolks, salt, lemon rind, and remaining flour. Knead well. Let rise until double, about two hours. On floured board, roll ¾ inch thick. Brush with 2 Tablespoons butter and sprinkle with sugar, cinnamon, and currants. Roll and cut into 1-inch slices. Mix brown sugar with remaining butter and spread on bottom of heavy skillet with ovenproof handle. Place dough circles on sugar, and let rise until double. Bake at 350 degrees 30 minutes or until well browned. Invert skillet over rack. Yields 1 dozen.

BURTON FOX INN PHEASANTS IN CREAM WITH APPLES

2 pheasants, 2 ½ to 3
  pounds each
4 Tablespoons butter
2 cups tart apples, peeled
  and chopped
½ cup + 1 Tablespoon
  applejack brandy

2 cups heavy cream
¼ cup lemon juice
Salt and white pepper
1 Tablespoon cornstarch

In heavy skillet, brown trussed pheasants in butter, remove, and keep warm. Saute apples in same skillet, spread in oven-proof casserole and place pheasants on top. Deglaze skillet with ½ cup applejack, scraping well. Pour over birds. Cover casserole and bake at 375 degrees 45 minutes. Add cream, lemon juice, and seasonings, and cook uncovered 30 minutes, basting occasionally, until tender. Remove birds to heated platter. Blend cornstarch with remaining applejack and stir into liquid in casserole. Cook over medium heat until thick, then strain over birds, and serve with wild rice. Serves 4.

BURTON FOX INN PANNEQUAIQUES

1 cup flour
1 Tablespoon sugar
¼ teaspoon salt
2 eggs + 2 yolks

1 ¾ cups milk
2 Tablespoons melted
  butter
1 teaspoon rum or cognac

In bowl or blender, combine all ingredients and beat until smooth. Spoon 1 Tablespoon batter into a greased, hot, 6-inch skillet, tilting to spread over bottom of pan. Cook until firm on bottom, about 1 ½ minutes, then turn to brown other side. Stack with waxed paper between to keep warm. Stuff each crêpe with creamed chicken or maple butter.

WELSHFIELD INN
Welshfield

Geauga, the Indian word for "raccoon," was the name chosen for this heavily forested county in which three important rivers rise. The Cuyahoga, the Chagrin, and the Grand (originally Geauga) add to its beauty, but their impassibility and the hilly terrain slowed industrial growth. No large towns developed, and travel was difficult until well into the nineteenth century.

In 1842, Alden J. Nash opened a hotel in the home of J.E. Sperry in the village of Welshfield; it was not long before he built a place of his own, and called it The Nash Hotel. A stopping point on the stagecoach route from Cleveland to Pittsburgh, it became a social center for residents as well, and was enlarged repeatedly during a succession of owners, acquiring a ballroom and a Mount Vernon-style portico.

In 1946, the inn came on the market, and Brian Holmes, just out of the army, and his wife Polly, a dietician, teamed with another couple to try their hands at innkeeping. Three years later, the Holmeses bought out their partners, and eventually gave up the overnight business, concentrating on the restaurant. Polly perfects the recipes, Brian is chef, and after forty years, their enthusiasm for their work still shows.

"There's romance in foods," Brian said. "People should be aware of these things and not just sit down and eat!"

Fresh flowers and lace tablecloths in the dining rooms create a grandmotherly, welcoming atmosphere at Welshfield Inn, and the East Room, part of the original 1840's structure, is still in use. New food ideas are brought home by Brian and Polly from their travels, and menus change according to season and availability.

"In Spring," Brian said, "we have fresh salmon from Washington state, and roast leg of spring lamb. The baker, who has been here twenty-four years, changes dessert menus according to season— cobblers and pies in summer, when we have access to a lot of local produce."

Welshfield Inn's remarkable cream of black olive soup is a good starter for any meal; luncheon entrées range from braised chicken livers on toast to Coquille St. Jacques, with potato or vegetable and salad. For dinner, you might try the Medallion of Tenderloin Saute, with mushrooms, tomatoes, onions and peppers, or one of the frequent fresh fish specials. Vegetables and rolls are hot and unusual, but save room for cheesecake with orange sauce, Galliano mousse, or yummy fruit cobblers.

Welshfield Inn is on Route 422 in Welshfield, 13 miles east of Chagrin Falls. Mailing address is 14001 Main-Market, Burton, Ohio 44021. Lunch, Tuesday through Saturday, is from 12 Noon to 2:30 p.m.; dinner Tuesday through Thursday is 5 to 8 p.m., Friday and Saturday to 9 p.m., and Sunday from 12 Noon to 8 p.m. The Inn is closed from December 24 to the last Friday in January, and the first two weeks in July. (216)834-4164. All legal beverages are served, including Sunday, attire is "Dressy casual," and reservations are encouraged, especially for parties of six or more. Children's prices are available. AE, CB, DC, MC, V. ($$)

WELSHFIELD INN HOT BUTTERED WINE

12 ounces frozen orange juice concentrate
4 cups water
¼ cup sugar
¼ teaspoon cinnamon
¼ teaspoon nutmeg
2 Tablespoons butter
⅕ gallon white wine

In large pot, blend all ingredients except wine and bring to boil. Add wine and heat, but do not boil.

WELSHFIELD INN HARVARD BEETS BURGUNDY

2 1-pound cans beets, tiny rosebud or shoestring
2 Tablespoons cornstarch
1 cup sugar
¼ teaspoon ground cloves
Dash salt
1 cup Burgundy or Claret wine
½ cup wine vinegar
4 Tablespoons butter or margarine

Drain beets, reserving liquid. In saucepan, mix dry ingredients; gradually add wine, vinegar, and ½ cup beet juice, stirring until smooth. Stir over medium heat until thickened and clear. Add butter and beets; remove from heat, cover and let stand 30 minutes. Reheat before serving. Serves 10 to 12.

WELSHFIELD INN GLAZED CARROTS

1 pound can carrots, sliced
  or whole
1 ½ cups pineapple juice
2 Tablespoons orange
  juice concentrate
2 Tablespoons lemon juice
½ cup sugar
¼ cup cornstarch

Drain carrots, reserving liquid. Combine all ingredients except cornstarch in saucepan and bring to boil. Thicken with 1 cup carrot liquid mixed with cornstarch. Add a little diced lemon and orange. Serve hot. Serves 6.

WELSHFIELD INN GALLIANO MOUSSE

1 Tablespoon gelatin
2 Tablespoons cold water
4 egg yolks
½ cup sugar
1 cup hot milk
½ teaspoon vanilla
1 cup heavy cream,
  whipped
½ cup Liquore Galliano
Apricots, fresh or canned,
  for garnish
Galliano Golden Fruit
  Sauce (see below)

Soften gelatin in water. In double boiler over simmering water, beat together yolks and sugar until very thick. Gradually stir in milk and vanilla, then softened gelatin. Strain. Cool, stirring occasionally. Fold in whipped cream and Galliano. Pour into 6 or 8 glasses or a quart mold, and chill four hours. Garnish with apricots and fruit sauce.

For Galliano Golden Fruit Sauce:

1 cup pineapple juice
¼ cup sugar
Juice of ½ lemon
1 Tablespoon cornstarch
2 Tablespoons frozen
  orange juice
  concentrate
¼ cup Liquore Galliano

In saucepan, combine juices and sugar and bring to boil. Blend cornstarch with concentrate and stir into boiling juice. Cook until slightly thickened and clear. Stir in Galliano and chill.

THE PERFECT MATCH
Mentor

When it was built in 1868, the Hart Nut and Washer Manufacturing Company's factory cost $11,500, and was used to make wagons, agricultural implements, and millwork, in addition to nuts and washers. Perhaps it was too diversified; the company ceased operations in 1879, and the sprawling red brick structure was used as a barrel factory and a cider mill, before it became the Mentor Knitting Mills.

Knitted underwear for the entire family was made here until 1916. Other occupants produced chemicals, animal medicines, and cloth bags, and in 1938, it became home of the Columbia Match Company, which made book matches and match-making machines until the 1970s.

Mentor's oldest factory was then purchased and renovated to house offices and an open, airy, and very unusual restaurant that occupies an entire wing.

"The Perfect Match," commemorates not only the building's longest tenants, but the restaurateur parents of Al Covert, who, with his wife Jeanene, opened the restaurant in 1984. They had made a lengthy search of the area for a location before settling on this one. "We felt it was one heck of a place to put a restaurant," Al said.

The wing was gutted; bulldozers created three different floor levels, but walls and beams were left intact. High-tech exposed ductwork and wiring are somehow made cozy with dark rose paint, skylights, lots of plants, and a fire in cool weather. There's a patio with its own menu for cookout summer meals, and wherever you sit, the effect is not at all factory-like.

And food such as this was never served in a factory lunchroom. It's what Covert calls "overportioned," but generosity is not the only key to success at The Perfect Match. Chef Rusty Chervin, in charge since the beginning, offers something to please every taste. The spinach in the salad is the crispest, the sandwiches are made with the freshest meats and cheeses, the beef is cut on the premises every day, and there are always fresh fish specials. Homemade, hot, potato chips are thin and crunchy, and exquisite desserts rival each other for praise.

The Perfect Match, 8500 Station Street, Mentor, Ohio 44060, is off Center Street (Ohio 615), near the railroad tracks. It is open Monday through

Thursday, 11 a.m. to 11 p.m., until 1 a.m. Friday and Saturday, with continuous service. (216)255-7320 and (216)255-7827. Dress is casual, all legal beverages are served, and reservations are accepted. A special menu is available for children or lighter appetites, and for Early Bird Specials served 4:30 to 6 p.m. at a reduced cost. AE, MC, V. ($$$)

PERFECT MATCH CHOCOLATE CHECKERBOARD CHEESECAKE

For crust: In blender or food processor, crush 36 chocolate wafers into fine crumbs. Blend in 1 stick cold butter and ¼ teaspoon cinnamon, using on/off turns. Press mixture firmly into bottoms of three 8 ½" round, disposable aluminum pans, and place in freezer.

For filling:

1 ½ pounds cream cheese, at room temperature
1 ¼ cups sugar
4 eggs, at room temperature
2 cups sour cream, at room temperature
2 ½ teaspoons vanilla
2 Tablespoons flour
4 ounces semisweet chocolate, melted and cooled
2 teaspoons cocoa

In large mixer bowl, beat cream cheese until fluffy. Blend in sugar, then 3 eggs, one at a time, scraping sides of bowl with spatula. Beat in sour cream and 1 ½ teaspoons vanilla. Divide batter in half. Return one half to mixer, and lightly beat in remaining egg and 1 teaspoon vanilla. Sift flour into mixture and beat in. Set aside. Return second half of batter to mixer. Beat in melted chocolate and cocoa. Set crust-lined pans into three 9" cake pans for stability. Place batter divider ring from checkerboard cake pan set into one lined pan. Spoon vanilla batter into middle ring, filling about ¾ full, and chocolate batter into outer and inner rings, filling about ¾ full. Smooth top of each layer with teaspoon. Remove divider very carefully, lifting straight up with slight jiggling motion. Rinse and dry divider thoroughly, place into second pan, and fill as for first pan. Rinse and dry divider again, place into third pan, and spoon vanilla batter into outer and inner rings, and chocolate into middle ring. Bake layers 30 minutes at 325 degrees. Turn off heat, and leave pans in oven 15 minutes. Open oven door and cool layers completely. Refrigerate layers until well chilled, or overnight. Freeze layers while preparing frosting.

For frosting: melt 1 pound Swiss milk chocolate over hot water; cool to room temperature, and whisk in 1 ⅓ cups sour cream until smooth, then 2 Tablespoons light crème de cocoa liqueur.

To assemble: remove cake layers from supporting pans, and cut disposable pans in several places with scissors. Bend sides down, insert spatula under crusts, and carefully remove layers to serving platter, crust side down, with chocolate, vanilla, and chocolate outer rings alternating, and a thin layer of frosting over each. Spoon remaining frosting onto cake, and spread evenly over top and sides. Serves 12.

THE PUFFERBELLY
Kent

The steam engine, already used to power riverboats, was proven feasible for railway trains in 1825. Ohio's first operating railroad, The Mad River and Lake Erie, linked with the Little Miami railway at Springfield in 1848, creating over 200 miles of rail transportation from Sandusky to Cincinnati.

The Civil War slowed the furious railroad construction of the 1850's, but by 1880 Ohio had over five thousand miles of tracks, belonging to seventy-three companies.

The Atlantic and Western Railway, completed in 1864, connected lines from New York to St. Louis, and brought new prosperity to the village renamed "Kent" for its organizer and first president, Marvin S. Kent. In 1875, Kent's new two-story brick railway depot, in the Italian Villa or Tuscan style, was the height of elegance; a hundred years later, abandoned and endangered, it was purchased by the Kent Historical Soci-

THE PUFFERBELLY
Berea

ety. With the Kent Industrial District, it was placed on the National Register in 1974.

The quarries of Berea provided the rugged sandstone for Berea's handsome depot in 1876; eighteen-foot ceilings, slate roof, and a forty-five-foot tower added distinction to a structure built by the Cleveland, Columbus, Cincinnati, and Indianapolis Railroad. It was placed on the National Register in 1980, and in that same year, became The Pufferbelly Restaurant. The Kent depot became another Pufferbelly in 1981.

These two historic depots, charmingly restored, are both on still-active railroad lines. Guests, seated among railroad memorabilia, may watch and listen to passing trains as they dine on foods that were unknown in Ohio when the stations were new.

Tom Roehl, who, with his architect partner, George Lewis, operates the Pufferbellies, wants them to be restaurants people patronize regularly, not just on special occasions.

"We don't look at our restaurants as museums," he said. "The real measure of any restaurant is its food and service.

51

I do like the ambience of a historic building— it makes a distinctive place to go."

Relying on careful buying of fresh fish, steaks, and local produce, Roehl presents interesting, unusual foods at moderate prices in both restaurants.

One all-day menu provides appetizers, salads, and "Hearty and Trendy" items such as quesidilla, quiches, omelets, stir-fried vegetables, and sandwiches— including a hollowed Kaiser roll filled with curried tuna topped with cheese and broiled. Dinner adds steaks, chicken, barbecued ribs, and elegances such as Shrimp and Peapods, or Veal Dijon Florentine.

Desserts are as simple as fresh strawberries sauced with sour cream, brown sugar and Amaretto, or as complex as crêpes filled with walnuts and raisins and topped with rum-flavored syrup. There's also a dense, sweet, peanut butter pie topped with whipped cream and drizzled with chocolate....

The Pufferbelly Restaurant, 30 Depot Street, Berea, Ohio 44017, is open 11 a.m. to 10 p.m. Monday through Thursday, until 12 midnight Friday and Saturday, with continuous service, and for Sunday dinner only, 4 to 9 p.m. (216)234-1144.

The Pufferbelly Restaurant, 152 Franklin Avenue, Kent, Ohio 44240, is open 11 a.m. to 10 p.m. Monday through Thursday, until 12 midnight Friday and Saturday, with continuous service, for Sunday brunch buffet 11 a.m. to 2:30 p.m., dinner 3 to 9 p.m. (216)673-1771. At both, dress is casual, reservations are accepted only for parties of eight or more, and all legal beverages are served, including Sunday. AE, MC, V. ($$)

PUFFERBELLY SOLE CROWN FLORENTINE

3 filets sole, 7 or 8 ounces each
Salt
1 cup Florentine stuffing (see below)

⅓ cup dry white wine
¼ teaspoon paprika
⅛ teaspoon pepper

Wash fish and pat dry, place skin side up and salt lightly. Place ⅓ cup stuffing in center of each filet. Roll up, securing with toothpick. Stand on end, "crown fashion," in greased baking pan. Pour wine over crowns, season, and bake at 325 degrees for 25 to 35 minutes, or until flaky. Do not overbake. 1 serving.

For Florentine stuffing:
1 ½ cups spinach, washed, drained, and chopped OR ¾ cup frozen spinach, thawed and drained
½ cup sour cream
½ cup cracker crumbs
2 ounces margarine
½ cup minced onions
4 ounces sliced mushrooms
1 ounce slivered almonds
Salt and pepper

Blend spinach with sour cream and crumbs. In skillet, melt margarine, add onions, mushrooms, and almonds, and stir until slightly cooked. Season, blend with spinach mixture, and chill. Yields 4 servings.

PUFFERBELLY SEA SCALLOPS SCANDINAVIAN

1 ounce butter
2 ounces flour
¼ teaspoon white pepper
¼ teaspoon paprika
5 ounces bay scallops
1 ounce Chablis wine
Mustard-dill sauce (see below)

In skillet, melt butter over low heat. Blend flour with spices, and dredge scallops, shaking off excess. Saute scallops in butter until opaque and crusted. Be gentle, and do not overcook. Add Chablis, and serve with stripe of mustard-dill sauce.

For mustard-dill sauce: blend one 7/8 ounce package Knorr-Swiss Hollandaise sauce mix, reconstituted according to package directions, with 2 ¼ teaspoons Dijon mustard and ½ teaspoon dill weed. Serves 6.

PUFFERBELLY BLACK FOREST COUPE

Semi-sweet chocolate cup
Black cherry ice cream
Raspberry sauce (see below)
Whipped cream

In chilled coupe glass or other serving dish, place chocolate cup; in cup place large scoop of ice cream, and pour 2 ounces sauce over. Decorate with whipped cream. Serves one.

For raspberry sauce: blend 16 ounces raspberry pie filling, 1 ounce Burgundy wine, and ½ ounce brandy with spatula. Store in covered container in refrigerator. Yields 8 servings.

BENDER'S TAVERN
Canton

Bezaleel Wells, a Baltimore native, settled Canton about 1805, and named it for a large estate near his Maryland home. He was joined by Pennsylvania Germans, whose industry made Canton a prosperous city of 1,500 people by 1830. A manufacturing town, its first products were farm implements and watches.

In a side street called "Whiskey Alley" for its numerous barrooms, a corner tavern was designed in 1899 by Guy Tilden, a well-known Canton architect. With six other structures designed by Tilden, it has been nominated for inclusion in the National Register of Historic Places.

An unassuming, two-story red brick building known as "The Belmont," it housed a tavern— possibly called "Hoffbrau Haus'— on the first floor, a brewery in the basement, and hotel rooms upstairs. Its exterior does not indicate the warmth and charm of the interior, where enormous stained glass windows, high marble wainscots, and dark wood paneling and ceiling beams create a European atmosphere.

The tavern, purchased in the early 1900s by Ed Bender, was expanded into an adjacent livery stable and barber shop, creating a dining room, a ladies' dining room, and a lunch counter.

About 1916, there was a general remodeling, but few changes have been made since that time. Bender's is a period restaurant well worth a visit, even if the food were not remarkable.

But it is.

A seafood house with a reputation for great steaks, Bender's is now operated by the third generation of one family. During the depression, Bender's closed briefly, and was reopened in 1932 by John Jacobs, a banker and former patron. His son "Wib,' and grandsons Jim and Jerry have continued the food tradition that has made Bender's one of the most popular and enduring restaurants in Ohio.

Seafood is shipped in from Boston, so the menu changes daily; some fish are prepared Cajun style, others are broiled, sautéed, or poached. USDA Prime steaks and prime rib are cut on the spot and generously served.

Bender's is also famous for fried-baked potatoes with crisp

edges, puffy middles, and real down-home flavor, and turtle soup, a rich brown concoction served with sherry.

Desserts range from Amish-baked pies to walnut delight and baklava from the Greek bakery that also bakes the delectable rolls, but most requested is Bender's own sundae, thickly blanketed in a luxuriant chocolate and peanut butter sauce.

Bender's Tavern, 137 Court Avenue S.W., Canton, Ohio 44702, is open Monday through Thursday from 11 a.m. to 10 p.m., until 11 p.m. Friday and Saturday, with continuous service. (216)453-8424. Dress is casual, although T-shirts and shorts are prohibited, and most men wear coats. All legal beverages are served, and there is an extensive wine list. Reservations are suggested. Breakfast is served one day only, for the Professional Football Hall of Fame Festival, usually the last weekend in July. AE, CB, MC, V. ($$$)

BENDER'S DEVILLED CRAB CAKES

2 Tablespoons + 2
   teaspoons melted butter
⅝ to ¾ cup flour
½ cup clam juice
¾ to 1 cup milk
¾ teaspoon cayenne
   pepper
2 drops Tabasco
¼ cup green pepper, finely
   diced

¼ cup scallions, finely
   diced
Butter for sautéeing
1 pound crabmeat, cleaned
¼ to ½ cup breadcrumbs
8 toast squares
Paprika

In pan, blend butter and flour and cook over medium heat about a minute; add clam juice and milk gradually to make a thick sauce. Remove from heat and add seasonings. In another pan, sauté green pepper and scallions in a little butter, then add to sauce with crabmeat and mix well. Blend in enough breadcrumbs to stiffen, and form into 5 ½ ounce balls. Place on a toast square, sprinkle with paprika, and bake 45 minutes at 325 degrees, until hot and solid. Serve with hot butter. Serves 8.

BENDER'S PICKEREL, CAMP KEGEL STYLE

Season the meat side of yellow pickerel filets with MSG and paprika, dust with flour, and place meat side down in very hot grease. When browned, flip over filets, and finish off in oven until done.

BENDER'S FROG LEGS, SAUTÉED WITH MUSHROOMS

Blend flour with salt, pepper, MSG, and paprika, and dust frog legs with the mixture. Saute in butter, adding a little extra flour. When frog legs are about half done, add chopped mushrooms, minced garlic, and stock. Cook until thickened, and add sherry wine to taste.

BENDER'S CRABMEAT FILLING FOR MUSHROOMS AND FLOUNDER

1 stick butter, melted
¾ cup + 1 Tablespoon flour
3 cups milk
¾ teaspoon salt
Pinch of white pepper
¾ teaspoon
  Worcestershire sauce
2 drops Tabasco
¾ teaspoon MSG
⅛ cup lemon juice
1 ¼ pounds crabmeat,
  cleaned

In pan, blend butter and flour and cook over medium heat about a minute; add milk gradually to make a sauce. Add seasonings and cook until thick; let cool and add crabmeat. For stuffed mushrooms, place this mixture in mushroom caps, sauté in butter, add brandy and bake in moderate oven until mushrooms are tender and filling is browned.

THE TAVERNE OF RICHFIELD
Richfield

Until the Ohio and Erie Canal came through the Portage Summit, the highest point on the canal, the region was one of small farms that produced wheat, sheep, and dairy products. Towns developed slowly, providing services and trading centers for outlying farms.

In 1809, Launcelot Mayes came to what is now the Village of Richfield. A few others moved into the area, but settlement was sparse until after the War of 1812, when newcomers arrived from Connecticut and Massachusetts. Forty voters were registered in 1816, and a Congregational church was built in 1818.

The population of Richfield Township had grown to 1253 people by 1880. Nearly every occupation was included, with some as esoteric as "carriage trimmer," indicating a wealthy clientele.

In Richfield, near the northwest corner of the public square, The West Richfield Hotel, a large, two-story frame structure, was built in 1886. Owned by Baxter Wood of Medina, and operated by Lewis P. Ellas, it featured an impressive two-story gallery with a decorative railing, and a bracketed hip roof enclosing a ballroom with a ceiling resembling an inverted ship's hull.

Many elaborate functions took place in the new hotel, but times change, and when restaurateur Mel Rose bought the building, it had been condemned.

"It took about six months construction and renovation," he said. "During that time, I collected antiques and furniture and fixtures to restore the building. Most are from Northeastern Ohio."

Surrounded by crystal chandeliers, walnut-framed mirrors, and stained glass indoors, or by lush, summer greenery in a brick courtyard outside, patrons of the Taverne of Richfield once again feast on elegant food. "We buy the highest quality food we can buy," Rose said. "If there's a problem with the food, it's something we've created."

But there are no problems; Chef Peter Girardin raises that quality food to superb heights. Soups, sandwiches, and salads, such as the enormous mound of fresh melon, pineapple, berries, apples and oranges in a cantaloupe shell, join light entrées for luncheon. In the evening, Taverne specialties of veal, lamb, duck, and seafoods increase an already generous listing. There's even a special menu for dieters, with food every bit as tasty and attractive.

From creative appetizers— the Hot Crabmeat Taverne Style is a winner, with scallions, mushrooms, and tomatoes in a cheesy Hollandaise— to desserts that range from Apple Walnut Pie oozing cinnamon and brown sugar to Mocha Chocolate Swirl Cheesecake, food at the Taverne of Richfield is generously served and beautifully presented.

The Taverne of Richfield, One Park Place, Richfield, Ohio 44286, where Ohio 176 intersects Ohio 303, is open for lunch 11:30 a.m. to 2:30 p.m. Monday through Saturday, for dinner 5 to 11 p.m., Monday through Thursday, until 12 Midnight Friday and Saturday. Sunday Brunch is 10:30 to 2:30, and dinner 3:30 to 10 p.m. (216)659-3155. Dress code requires jackets for men, and all legal beverages are served, including Sunday after 1 p.m. Reservations are preferred, and are almost a necessity on weekends, during the month of December and events at the Coliseum, and for large parties. Children's menu is available. AE, CB, DC, MC, V. ($$$)

TAVERNE OF RICHFIELD SALAD
TAVERNE STYLE

1 head Boston or Bibb lettuce	2 artichoke hearts, halved
½ cup mushrooms, sliced	1 scallion, cut in ½" pieces
2 hearts of palm, cut in ¾" pieces	3 slices avocado
	4 cherry tomatoes

Wash and drain lettuce. Core and remove outside leaves. Arrange remaining leaves in flower pattern on 8" salad plate. Distribute ingredients over lettuce attractively. Serve with Green Goddess or Italian dressing. One serving.

TAVERNE OF RICHFIELD DUCK A L'ORANGE

Two 5-pound ducks
2 Tablespoons salt
2 celery stalks, halved
2 carrots, halved
½ onion, cut in half
2 Tablespoons rosemary

2 teaspoons white pepper
2 cups sliced apples
2 cups raisins
½ cup brown sugar
¼ cup white wine
Orange glaze (see below)

Rub cavity of each duck with salt; divide celery, carrots, and onion into cavities. Sprinkle rosemary and pepper over ducks and roast in 350 degree oven 3 hours. In saucepan, combine apples and raisins and heat five minutes. Add sugar and wine, stirring until combined, and serve under duck. Garnish with parsley, and orange slices marinated in Grand Marnier, and serve with orange glaze. Serves 4.

For orange glaze: Thicken orange juice with cornstarch to desired consistency, add Cointreau or Grand Marnier, and cook for five minutes.

THE TAVERNE OF RICHFIELD CURRIED FRUITS

16 ounce can peach halves, drained
16 ounce can pear halves, drained
16 ounce can pineapple chunks, drained
16 ounce can pitted dark sweet cherries, drained

1 stick + 2 teaspoons margarine
⅓ cup brown sugar, packed
2 ½ teaspoons curry powder

Arrange fruit in baking pan. In saucepan, melt sugar and margarine and pour over fruit. Sprinkle with curry powder and bake in 350 degree oven 30 minutes, stirring once. Refrigerate overnight. To serve, heat desired amount, including at least one of each fruit. Place in serving dish, and top with cinnamon-flavored whipped cream.

THE WATERMARK
Cleveland

In May of 1795, most of the land in Connecticut's Western Reserve was offered for sale, and The Connecticut Land Company, representing fifty people in Hartford, bought 120 miles of Lake Erie shore for about thirty-five cents an acre. Moses Cleaveland, a company director, headed a party of pioneers and surveyors who reached the mouth of the Cuyahoga River on July 22, 1796, where they laid out a town named for their leader.

A trading post some ten years earlier had failed; Cleaveland's would-be settlers, exhausted from malaria and the rigorous journey, also gave up. Only three of the original band stayed on the river the Indians called "Crooked."

Growth was slow. In 1810, the population was fifty-seven; in 1825, when it was chosen as the northern terminus of the Ohio and Erie Canal, there were 606 people and fifty houses.

Immigrants who came to build the canal stayed to man industries; iron ore, coal, and timber were readily available, and manufacturing and shipping increased. When the canal was completed in 1832, population had doubled.

As the town grew, its name was shortened. The first "a" in Cleaveland was dropped, according to legend, by an editor who could not fit the entire name on his paper's masthead.

Only a few hundred feet from Moses Cleaveland's landing, in an area of warehouses and small industries called "The Flats," a ships' chandlery was built after the Civil War by butcher Louis Hausheer, who provided fresh foods to lake schooners. His handsome iron-fronted building became The Watermark Restaurant in the fall of 1985.

The soaring ceiling provides a spectacular view of river activity; in summer, a patio extends seating to water's edge. Freighters and pleasure craft maneuver under bridges, and gulls swoop down for dinner, while The Watermark's patrons devour more sophisticated seafood.

"We specialize in fresh seafood," said Hap Gray, general manager. "We buy widely available, good fresh ingredients and pass the savings along to the customer."

Attracted by Chef Michele Gaw's innovative preparation, The Watermark's clientele enjoys traditional foods with a twist: Caesar Salad with salmon; smoked chicken salad in pita; and a flaky Seafood Strudel head a list of seafoods that are grilled, baked, pan-fried, and blackened.

The Seafood Bar offers clams, mussels, oysters, shrimp, and daily specials for those in a hurry; steaks, chicken, and veal are among non-seafood choices. As counterpoint to a low-fat meal, scrumptious hot breads and rich desserts provide all the decadence you could wish.

The Watermark, 1250 Old River Road, Cleveland, Ohio 44113, is open for lunch 11:30 a.m. to 2:30 p.m. every day (Sunday brunch same hours), and for dinner 5:30 to 10 p.m. Sunday through Thursday, 5:30 to 12 Midnight Friday and Saturday. Seafood bar is open 11 a.m. to 1 a.m., with continuous service. (216)241-1600. Dress code prohibits "cut-off" shorts, T-shirts, motorcycle jackets, and work boots. All legal beverages are served, including Sunday, and there is an extensive wine list. Reservations are recommended, especially Saturday night, often booked weeks ahead. AE, CB, DC, MC, V, Discover. ($$$)

THE WATERMARK SWORDFISH IN LEMON GINGER MARINADE

Six 8-ounce swordfish steaks (less than one inch thick to avoid burning on charcoal grill)

Place steaks in shallow pan and cover with marinade. Refrigerate 2 hours. Grill over medium heat, five minutes on each side. Serves 6.

For marinade:
½ cup lemon juice
1 teaspoon minced lemon zest
2 medium garlic cloves, minced
1 ½ teaspoons minced fresh ginger

2 Tablespoons olive oil
2 Tablespoons oil
¼ teaspoon salt
⅛ teaspoon pepper

Combine marinade ingredients and whisk until blended. Note: lime juice and zest may be substituted for lemon, and any firm-fleshed fish (shark, tuna, halibut, etc.) for swordfish.

THE WATERMARK APRICOT BREAD

6 ounces dried apricots	3 cups flour
2 ounces butter	2 teaspoons baking soda
1 ½ cups sugar	½ teaspoon salt
2 eggs, beaten	1 cup chopped nuts

Cover apricots with 1 cup boiling water and let stand 15 minutes. Cream butter and sugar; add eggs, apricots, and water. Mix dry ingredients and blend into apricot mixture. Add nuts. Divide into 2 greased 9″ x 5″ x 3″ loaf pans. Bake at 350 degrees for 45 to 60 minutes.

THE WATERMARK PUMPKIN CHEESECAKE WITH SHORTBREAD CRUST

Shortbread crust:

1 ½ cups flour	1 egg, beaten
¼ to ⅓ cup sugar	½ cup butter
Pinch of salt	

In large bowl, mix ingredients with hands, then press into bottom of 11-inch springform pan and pierce with fork. Bake for 15 minutes at 400 degrees. Cool.

Filling:

2 ½ pounds cream cheese	1 teaspoon ground cloves
1 cup sugar	1 teaspoon ground ginger
4 large eggs, beaten	1 cup heavy cream
3 egg yolks, beaten	1 Tablespoon vanilla
3 Tablespoons flour	1 pound mashed, cooked
2 teaspoons cinnamon	pumpkin

In large mixer bowl, beat together cheese, sugar, eggs, and yolks. Add flour and spices, cream and vanilla. Add pumpkin and beat until just mixed. Pour mixture into cool crust and bake 15 minutes at 375 degrees. Reduce heat to 225 degrees and bake another hour. Turn off heat, but leave cheesecake in oven overnight to cool. Serve warm or chilled, with whipped cream.

OHIO CITY TAVERN
Cleveland

In 1836, on the west bank of the Cuyahoga, a village called "City of Ohio" was incorporated. It was known as "Ohio City," despite its official name, and attracted successful businesses and handsome dwellings from its inception, reaching a population of over 1500 in 1840. Fiercely competitive with Cleveland, the town opposed construction of a bridge over the Cuyahoga, fearing that trade would bypass it in favor of its neighbor. After Cleveland won the "Bridge War," both cities prospered, and the two were united in 1854.

A corner tavern built of rose-colored brick in 1867 has been in service to Ohio City residents and visitors ever since; during World War I and prohibition, it was a grocery and laundry. In 1972, the building was restored, with additions of a larger kitchen and enclosed patio. With the Ohio City Preservation District, the Ohio City Tavern was placed on the National Register in 1974.

Owned since 1978 by Paul Prasse and Ronald Gogul, its outstanding staff has made it one of Cleveland's favorite places: Ann Fulcomer, head chef, also creates the rich home-made ice creams; Sam Gliozzi, assistant chef, is responsible for the superb pastries; and Carlos Colon is general manager.

Some interior additions were made around the turn of the century, when the back bar was added and the paneling installed. Stained glass from demolished St. Mary's church was mounted on the dining room ceiling in 1972; later, upstairs rooms became private dining rooms. There's al fresco dining in the courtyard in summer, and a wood-burning fire in winter.

Ohio City Tavern's food relies on fresh seafoods and beef, plus popular Cajun specials and veal, creatively prepared. Appetizers— the Artichoke Parmesan, a hot salad, is delightful— are plentiful, including baked Brie and Calimari. Entrées are creative: Cajun Shrimp Diane is a variation of Steak Diane, and Spanish Veal has pimiento and capers in a sherry cream sauce.

Desserts— ice creams, tortes, and cheesecakes with liqueurs, trifles and fruit mousses— change every day, and are enough to tempt even those without a sweet tooth!

Ohio City Tavern, 2801 Bridge Avenue, Cleveland, Ohio 44113, is open for lunch 11 a.m. to 3 p.m. Monday through Friday, until 4 p.m. Saturday, and for dinner 5:30 through 10 p.m. Monday through Thursday, until 11 p.m. Friday and Saturday. A bar menu from 3 to 5:30 p.m. provides continuous service. (216)687-0505. Attire is "Dressy casual," all legal beverages are served, and reservations are preferred. AE, CB, DC, MC, V. ($$$)

OHIO CITY TAVERN HIGHLAND CHICKEN

Four 8-ounce boned, skinned chicken breasts
Flour for dredging
½ cup butter
2 bunches scallions, chopped
½ cup slivered almonds

4 ounces Scotch whisky
½ teaspoon salt
½ teaspoon white pepper
1 cup heavy cream
1 pound spinach, cleaned and dried

Cut chicken breasts into 10 strips each. Dip in flour and shake off excess. In skillet, melt butter; sauté chicken, scallions, and almonds four minutes. Add whisky and flambé; when Scotch is burned, add seasonings and cream. Sauté two more minutes. Tear up spinach, divide onto heated plates, and pour chicken and sauce over spinach. Serves 4 to 6.

OHIO CITY TAVERN CRAB TWINS

1 ½ pounds crabmeat in small chunks
1 cup mayonnaise
8 ounces cream cheese
3 scallions, chopped
1 stalk celery, chopped
3 Tablespoons lemon juice
1 Tablespoon garlic powder

½ teaspoon pepper
1 teaspoon salt
1 teaspoon paprika
1 Tablespoon mustard
1 Tablespoon horseradish
12 large tomato slices
6 English muffins, split, buttered, and toasted
12 slices Provolone cheese

In large bowl, mix first 12 ingredients well. Place tomato slice on each ½ muffin, top with generous serving of crab mixture, then with cheese. On baking sheet, bake at 350 degrees 15 to 20 minutes, or until cheese is browned. Serves 6.

OHIO CITY TAVERN CHOCOLATE CHOCOLATE CHOCOLATE CHIP WALNUT CHEESECAKE

Chocolate crumb crust:

1 ½ cups fine breadcrumbs
¼ cup cocoa
10 Tablespoons sugar

1 teaspoon cinnamon
9 Tablespoons melted butter

Mix all ingredients. Press on bottom and sides of buttered 10″ springform pan. Refrigerate while making filling.

Chocolate filling:

2 pounds cream cheese, softened
10 eggs
3 Tablespoons flour
1 teaspoon vanilla

2 ½ cups sugar
1 cup cocoa
12 ounces chocolate chips
1 cup broken walnut meats
¼ cup heavy cream

In large mixer bowl, cream cheese. Add eggs one at a time, blending well, then remaining ingredients. Beat very smooth. Pour into prepared pan and bake at 350 degrees one hour and 20 minutes or until cake tester comes out slightly moist. Turn off oven, open door slightly, and let cheesecake cool one hour.

Chocolate topping: Whip 3 cups heavy cream with ½ cup powdered sugar and ¼ cup cocoa until stiff. Spread well-cooled cheesecake with ½ mixture. Using pastry bag, pipe remaining cream on cake. Decorate with walnut halves and shaved chocolate. Refrigerate.

DON'S POMEROY HOUSE
Strongsville

When John Stoughton Strong left Marlboro, Vermont, in 1816, he was forty-five years old, married, with a large family. He and his eldest son, Emory, journeyed to the Western Reserve, where he had purchased several thousand acres for about $2.50 an acre, and was empowered to sell additional acreage for the owners. A man of great energy, he helped to establish and settle the town which was named for him.

Among the earliest families in the area were the Popes and Pomeroys, both from Massachusetts. Alanson Pomeroy married Kezia Pope, and her brother Philander married his sister Lucy. Alanson was a successful businessman; he built and operated Strongsville's general store, was involved with several banks, and served as Justice of the Peace, a town trustee of Strongsville, and Postmaster.

In 1848, he built a two-story brick residence, called "The Homestead," in the Western Reserve Greek Revival style. A one-story wing on the south served as his office, and his store was diagonally across the street.

The Pomeroys were known for their hospitality, inviting distant members of the Congregational Church (built by Alanson Pomeroy) to Sunday lunch so they could stay for the second service. The house, a stop on the Underground Railroad, was occupied by members of the Pomeroy family until 1963. Despite its abandoned condition, residents recognized its importance, and it was placed on the National Register in 1975.

Restoration was begun in 1979 by Homestead Associates, owners of the property, who carefully returned the house to original condition and adapted it for use as a restaurant. A new west wing housing kitchens and a "library" dining room is beautifully matched to the original structure; parlor, dining room, and Judge Pomeroy's office now serve as intimate dining areas. Dark woodwork is set off by floral Victorian wallpapers, lace curtains shield tall windows, and guests once again enjoy hospitality at The Homestead, now Don's Pomeroy House.

Seafood is a specialty here, with daily shipments from Boston prepared to enhance their freshness, or to your request. Luncheon salads, egg and cheese dishes, pastas, and half-pound burgers are added to "Don's Freshline" of seafoods, and at dinner, there are Angus steaks, veal, and poultry as well. Desserts, like the seafoods, change daily, but are of equal quality, and are uniformly delicious.

Don's Pomeroy House, 13664 Pearl Road, Strongsville, Ohio 44136, is open for lunch 11 a.m. to 2:30 p.m., Monday through Friday, for dinner 5 to 10 p.m., Monday through Thursday, until 12 Midnight Friday and Saturday. Sunday Dinner is 4 to 9 p.m. In the basement Pub, hours are 11:30 a.m. to 1 a.m., with continuous service, including Saturday lunch. (216)572-1111. Patio and Pub dress is casual; no shorts or jeans are allowed inside. Most men wear coats and ties in the dining rooms. All legal beverages are served, reservations are accepted, required on Saturday evenings and for parties over five, and children's portions are available. AE, CB, DC, MC, V. ($$$)

DON'S POMEROY HOUSE POMEROY SALAD

2 ounces head lettuce
1 ounce Bibb lettuce
1 ounce spinach leaves
½ ounce purple onion rings

1 ounce Mandarin orange segments
2 strawberries OR sliced kiwi

Prepare lettuces, combine with spinach, and toss to mix. Place on serving plate, top with onion, and ring with oranges and strawberries or kiwi. Serve with a honey poppyseed dressing. One serving.

DON'S POMEROY HOUSE CORNISH GAME HEN WITH SAUSAGE HAZELNUT DRESSING AND WHISKEY HUNTER SAUCE

2 Cornish game hens, halved, breast and back bones removed; reserve necks and giblets for sauce

1 Tablespoon salt
1 Tablespoon white pepper
¼ teaspoon sage
4 strips bacon

Mix seasonings in bowl and rub inside and outside of bird. Lay bacon over breast and bake at 350 degrees for 1 hour.

For sausage hazelnut dressing:

1 cup diced celery	1 cup hazelnuts
1 onion, diced	2 eggs
½ cup diced green pepper	1 teaspoon salt
½ cup diced sweet red pepper	1 teaspoon sage
4 slices bread, diced	½ teaspoon celery salt
1 pound mild Italian sausage	¾ teaspoon white pepper
Oil for sautéeing nuts	3 dashes Tabasco
	4 dashes Worcestershire sauce

In large bowl, place vegetables and bread. In large skillet, sauté sausage, drain, and add meat to mixture. In a skillet with a little hot oil, place hazelnuts and fry until aromatic. Rub red skin off with a cloth, dice, and add to mixture. Add eggs and seasonings. Spread in baking dish and bake at 350 degrees for 30 minutes, with buttered waxed paper on top.

For Whiskey Hunter Sauce:

Reserved necks and giblets from hens	1 teaspoon white pepper
1 carrot, cut in 3 pieces	½ teaspoon garlic
1 rib celery	Pinch of ground Thyme
1 onion, halved	½ teaspoon sugar
½ cup whiskey	Roux of equal parts butter and flour blended to a paste
½ cup veal stock	
1 teaspoon salt	

Drain drippings from hens. Deglaze pan, and add juices to small pot with 2 cups cold water, giblets, and vegetables. Boil until reduced by half. Add whiskey, stock, and seasonings, and again reduce by half. Thicken with bits of roux, and strain. To serve: pour pool of sauce on plate. Mold dressing in coffee cup and place on plate, place hen halves crosswise, and garnish with daisy, green onion, and fluted mushroom. Serves 4.

THE OLD WAREHOUSE RESTAURANT
Roscoe Village, near Coshocton

On July 4, 1825, New York's Governor De Witt Clinton, known as "Father of the Erie Canal," turned the first spadeful of dirt on the Ohio and Erie Canal. By the time it was open to the Ohio River in 1832, a distance of 308 miles, farmers in Northeastern Ohio had already begun to profit from grain shipped to New York on the "big ditch.'

Water routes had always provided the fastest and most economical transportation for freight; on the Erie Canal, shipping costs were cut by eighty per cent, and time in transit reduced by two-thirds. Ohio gambled nearly $8 million, nine years, and the lives of countless laborers on the Ohio and Erie Canal, and the investment paid off in many ways.

Largely due to Ohio's canal system and The National Road, the state's population trebled in less than twenty years. Canalside villages flourished, industry grew, and farmers prospered.

At the junction of the Ohio and Erie and Walhonding canals, Roscoe became a wheat depot and commercial center. A foundry, cooperage, pottery, mills, and retail shops were built, a brickyard provided materials for the rapidly growing town, and a warehouse was constructed to store goods awaiting shipment.

As the canal era ended, businesses in Roscoe were gradually abandoned, and people moved away. In 1968, when Coshocton businessman Edward Montgomery and his wife, Frances, began restoration of the village, it had deteriorated, but was otherwise little changed in a hundred years.

The old warehouse, built in 1838 by Arnold Medbery, became a family restaurant in 1969, spearheading a restoration project that now boasts five canal-era exhibit buildings, horse-drawn canal boat and trolley rides, quaint shops in Greek Revival buildings, and lovely gardens. Interpreters in 1830's dress demonstrate weaving, pottery, and blacksmithing, and explain the day-to-day life of the period and the working of canal locks. The village was placed on the National Register in 1973.

There's always something fun going on in Roscoe Village, with a festival every warm-weather month and a big, old-fashioned Christmas. At any season, The Johnson-Humrickhouse Museum has an outstanding collection of Indian, Oriental, and American decorative arts.

A break in a busy and interesting day in Roscoe might include lunch in the spacious Old Warehouse Restaurant, where sunlight filters through shutters to gleam on glassware, and the quiet is restful.

Here, homey twentieth-century favorites are carefully prepared and attractively served. Try the Country Style Chicken Pot Pie, topped with delicate crisp pastry; an Old Fashioned Meat Loaf Sandwich; or Fresh Baked Ham with pineapple. At dinner, steaks, fried shrimp, and broiled orange roughy are added to the menu of salads and hearty sandwiches. At either meal, ice creams made in the village compete for your attention with homemade cheesecakes and deliciously rich pies: flaky homemade crusts surrounding some of the best fillings anywhere. If you can't choose between the peanut butter and lemon sour cream, have both!

The Old Warehouse Restaurant, 400 North Whitewoman Street, Coshocton, Ohio 43812, is open 11 a.m. to 8 p.m., with continuous service, except January through March, when Sunday through Thursday hours are 11 a.m. to 2:30 p.m. (614)622-9310. Dress is casual, all legal beverages are served (except Sunday) and reservations are required only for groups of 15 or more. A children's menu is available. AE, MC, V. ($$)

THE OLD WAREHOUSE BRAN MUFFINS

One 16-ounce box bran flakes	2 teaspoons salt
3 cups sugar	4 eggs, beaten
5 cups flour	1 cup vegetable oil
5 teaspoons soda	1 quart buttermilk

Mix dry ingredients, add eggs and liquids, and blend well. This mixture will keep in the refrigerator for up to 6 weeks. Fill greased muffin tins half full, and bake at 375 degrees for 15 minutes. Makes 3 dozen large muffins.

THE OLD WAREHOUSE CELERY SEED DRESSING

1 Tablespoon chopped
  onion
2 Tablespoons + 1
  teaspoon sugar
2 Tablespoons + 1
  teaspoon vinegar

½ teaspoon celery seed
½ teaspoon salt
½ teaspoon pepper
1 teaspoon dry mustard
1 cup vegetable oil

In blender, mix all ingredients except vegetable oil. When well combined, slowly add oil. Yields 1 ½ cups.

THE OLD WAREHOUSE PEANUT BUTTER PIE

One 9-inch pie shell, baked
¼ cup cornstarch
⅔ cup sugar
¼ teaspoon salt
2 cups milk, scalded
3 egg yolks, beaten

2 teaspoons butter
1 teaspoon vanilla
Crunchies (see below)
Whipped cream for
  topping

Cook all ingredients over medium heat, stirring, until thick. Remove from heat and cool slightly. Sprinkle half the crunchies on bottom of pie shell, pour in filling, and top with remaining crunchies. Chill, and serve topped with whipped cream.

For crunchies: Stir together 1 cup powdered sugar and ½ cup peanut butter until crumbly.

THE OLD WAREHOUSE LEMON SOUR CREAM PIE

One 9-inch pie shell, baked
1 cup sugar
3 Tablespoons cornstarch
1 Tablespoon grated
  lemon rind
¼ cup margarine

¼ cup lemon juice
1 cup milk
3 egg yolks, beaten
1 cup sour cream
Whipped cream for
  topping

Cook all ingredients but creams over medium heat until thick. Cool, and add sour cream. Pour into pie shell and chill 2 hours. Serve topped with whipped cream.

BUXTON INN
Granville

In the early 1800s, New England was plagued with overpopulation and exhausted soil, and westward migration seemed the only answer. Residents of Granville, Massachusetts, were encouraged by the success of former Granby, Connecticut, neighbors, who established Worthington, Ohio, in 1803.

As The Licking Land Company, a group of 107 men bought 26,000 acres in Ohio in February, 1805, and sent men to survey and plant crops for the fall harvest. In August, twenty-six families followed, eventually transplanting a New England town to the lovely wooded valley.

Early emphasis on religion and education is reflected in Granville's fine churches, and Dennison University, dating from 1831, overlooks the town from one of the adjacent hills. Nearly every nineteenth-century architectural style is exhibited on the shady streets of this exceptional village, where 119 structures are on the National Register of Historic Places.

In 1812, Orrin Granger built a two-story tavern of black walnut, in a style typical of the Connecticut River Valley. Serving as post office, stagecoach inn, and social center for the village, the L-shaped structure was large for its time, with a forty-foot frontage and a depth of sixty-four feet. A small east wing added about 1820, and a rear wing, ca. 1850, provided additional dining and overnight rooms, and formed a charming courtyard.

Under different names and owners, the tavern hosted many famous people, and was finally named "The Buxton Inn" for a longtime proprietor. Purchased in 1972 by former teachers Orville and Audrey Orr, who painstakingly researched its restoration, it was placed on the National Register in December, 1972.

Buxton Inn's peach-colored exterior iced with white was a popular New England choice of the period, and careful sanding proved it to have been the Inn's original color. Indoors, dining and overnight rooms are decorated with antiques appropriate to their period. Meals are served in the courtyard in warm weather, and before open fires in winter, presented by waitresses in early nineteenth century dress.

The American/French menu offers imaginative entrees: Veal

Sweetbreads with Burgundy Mushroom Sauce; Louisiana Chicken with Artichoke Hearts and Toasted Almonds; Buxton Sizzling Filet (with mushrooms, onion, and green pepper); all served with fresh vegetables.

Lighter luncheon fare includes sandwiches and salads, as does the separate Tavern menu, which has a Tex-Mex flavor. Desserts such as Three Chocolate Mousse Cake, prepared by Orville's mother, Gingerbread with Hot Lemon Sauce, and an enormous Peach Melba top off a memorable meal.

The Buxton Inn, 313 E. Broadway, Granville, Ohio 43023, is open 6:45 to 9 a.m. Monday through Friday, and 9 to 11 a.m. Saturday and Sunday, for breakfast; 11:30 a.m. to 2 p.m. for Monday through Saturday lunch and Sunday brunch; and 5:30 to 9 p.m. Monday through Thursday, 5:30 to 10 p.m. Friday and Saturday, and 12 Noon to 9 p.m. Sunday for dinner. Three rooms in the main building and 12 in nearby Warner House are available for overnight stays. (614)587-0001. Dress is casual to formal; most men wear coats and ties. All legal beverages are served (except Sunday), and reservations are suggested, almost imperative on weekends. AE, MC, V. ($$$)

BUXTON INN BLACK MUSHROOM SOUP

1 pound mushrooms, finely chopped
2 quarts chicken stock
1 medium onion, finely diced
2 small bay leaves
¼ teaspoon white pepper
½ cup sherry wine
½ pint whipping cream, whipped

Place first 6 ingredients in a 3-quart pot; bring to a boil, reduce heat, and simmer 15 minutes. Adjust seasoning. Serve topped with spoonful of unflavored whipped cream, garnished with fresh chopped chives OR dash of nutmeg. Serves 8.

BUXTON INN COQUILLE OF SEAFOOD

1 pound bay scallops
1 pound shelled, deveined
  small shrimp
¾ cup sherry wine
½ teaspoon salt
¼ teaspoon white pepper
1 bay leaf
2 Tablespoons minced
  scallions
½ pound cooked
  crabmeat, flaked

¼ cup chopped pimiento
2 cups sliced mushrooms,
  sautéed
Basic white sauce (see
  below)
Mayonnaise
Grated Parmesan cheese
Paprika

Place first 7 ingredients in saucepan with water to cover. Simmer 5 minutes and drain, reserving liquid. Reduce liquid to 1 cup and hold for white sauce. Add crab, pimiento and mushrooms to scallop mixture. Divide mixture among 12 coquille shells and top with a blend of equal parts white sauce and mayonnaise, sealing edges completely. Sprinkle with cheese and paprika, and bake at 400 degrees for 10 minutes or until top is brown and bubbly. Serves 6.

Basic white sauce:
¼ pound butter
¼ cup flour
¼ cup sherry wine
1 pint half-and-half cream
1 pint whipping cream
¼ cup reserved liquid (see
  above)

⅛ cup chicken base or
  bouillon granules
½ teaspoon onion powder
½ teaspoon garlic powder
Dash of white pepper
⅛ teaspoon thyme
½ teaspoon lemon juice

Stir butter and flour in small pan over low heat until a roux is formed. Do not brown. Combine liquids and spices in top of double boiler and bring to the boiling point. Add roux, stirring constantly, until thickened.

BRYN MAWR
Granville

Like many ambitious young men in the early nineteenth century, Elias Fassett saw the potential of the developing west. He left Vermont for Granville in 1818, at the age of twenty-one, and his financial skills assured his rapid success. In 1823, already one of the leading businessmen in the county, he married Jerusha Munson, of Granville's wealthiest family.

Fassett's business interests drew him to Cleveland and New York, but in 1849, as president of the Central Ohio Railroad, he returned to Granville and began construction of a large Italianate house south of town. The three-year project, called "Fassett's Folly" by villagers, included solid brick walls, a thirdfloor ballroom, and a square cupola on the roof, from which Fassett could oversee his railroad.

Fassett died in 1854, and the property passed through several owners, acquiring the name "Bryn Mawr" (pronounced brin maur), meaning "big hill" in Welsh, about 1890, and the Colonial Revival portico and balcony some time after 1911.

Bryn Mawr served as a girls' school, a school for the mentally retarded, and a nursing home, before being renovated as a restaurant in 1973. It was placed on the National Register in 1983.

Today, painted a warm yellow, Bryn Mawr is grounded in spectacular plantings of impatiens and geraniums, with permanent sunshine on the terrace under a yellow and white awning. Interiors are elegant in shades of cream and green, with plants in bay windows and flowers and crystal chandeliers reflected in handsome mirrors. In "Dave's Dig," the former summer kitchen and laundry in the basement, the atmosphere is less formal, and nightly entertainment is provided by Mike Williams, at his Bösendorfer piano.

Owners David and Dottie Klauder and Manager Philomena Dolen are proud of their restaurant, and of the shops on the lane, where crafts, antiques, plants, and herbs are offered to complete a country outing. "When people come to Bryn Mawr," David said, "They come for more than food— they come for the atmosphere and the country ambience."

But the food is equally special. An "eclectic" cuisine— American, with some Continental items— depends on the freshest meats, seafoods, and vegetables.

Favorites include homemade cinnamon rolls, Three Onion Soup (white and Bermuda onions and leeks, topped with melted Gruyere), and salmon in parchment with julienne vegetables. A good luncheon choice is Chicken Pot Pie, with lots of chicken and crisp-tender veggies under a golden puff paste crust. For dessert, try fresh fruit pie or warm apple dumpling in season, or, if you're not driving, one of the marvelous "Bartender" pies.

Bryn Mawr, 3758 Lancaster Road, Granville, Ohio 43023, is about 2 miles south of town on Ohio 37, 9 miles north of exit 126 off I-70. It is open for lunch 11:30 a.m. to 1:30 p.m. Monday through Friday, for dinner 5:30 to 9 p.m. Monday through Thursday, until 9:30 Friday and Saturday. Sunday brunch is served in seatings at 11 a.m. and 12:30 p.m., Sunday dinner is 4 to 7 p.m. During January, February, and March, Monday lunch and Sunday dinner are not served. (614)587-4000. Most men wear coats and ties, all legal beverages are served, including Sunday, and reservations are suggested, required on Sunday, and always helpful for parties of 6 or more. AE, MC, V, personal checks. ($$$)

BRYN MAWR SMOKED TROUT MOUSSE WITH DILL SAUCE

2 teaspoons unflavored
  gelatin
1 cup warm water
1 pound smoked trout,
  skin and bones removed

¾ cup mayonnaise
White pepper
Dill sauce (see below)

Dissolve gelatin in water. Purée trout in food processor or blender. Blend in mayonnaise, pepper to taste, and dissolved gelatin, and process to allow air to incorporate into mix. Pour into serving dish and refrigerate for one hour. Serve with Melba toast and dill sauce. Serves 6.

For dill sauce: Blend 1 cup sour cream, 1 Tablespoon dill weed, and ⅛ cup dill pickle juice. Chill.

Note: Other smoked fish may be substituted for trout.

BRYN MAWR DUCHESS SOUP

8 large carrots, peeled and
  grated
6 Tablespoons butter
6 Tablespoons flour
1 cup hot chicken broth

4 cups hot milk
2 pounds Cheddar cheese,
  grated
Salt and pepper to taste

Cook carrots in butter until soft. Stir in flour, then chicken broth and milk. Stir in cheese until melted, and season with salt and pepper. Serves 6.

BRYN MAWR CHICKEN AND CRAB

6 double chicken breasts,
  skinned and boned
2 Tablespoons butter
4 ounces white wine,
  divided
12 ounces Alaskan king OR
snow crab meat

Sauce (see below)
6 ounces toasted sliced
  almonds for garnish
18 blanched snow pea pods
  for garnish

Lay chicken in buttered baking dish, top with butter and 2 ounces wine, and bake at 350 degrees about 15 minutes or until chicken is firm. Heat crab meat in 2 ounces wine, place on 6 plates, and cover each with a chicken breast, top with sauce, and garnish with toasted almonds and pea pods. Serves 6.

For sauce:
1 cup milk
1 cup chicken broth
¼ cup butter

¼ cup flour
Salt and white pepper to
  taste

Heat milk and broth in saucepan; do not boil. Melt butter in saucepan, stir in flour, and add hot liquid gradually, stirring until smooth. Season with salt and pepper.

ENGINE HOUSE NO.5
Columbus

In the days of horse-drawn fire engines, a fire house was an exciting, complicated place. On one site, ready to answer calls in a hurry, were men, engines, horses, clothing and equipment, and hundreds of feet of hose.

The first mechanically operated fire engines, utilizing steam for power, were developed in the nineteenth century. Drawn by firemen or horses, steam fire engines were in a state of high development by the 1870s.

Many more fire houses were required then than in modern times. It took time to harness horses and drive them through narrow streets, and response time was crucial.

Engine House No.5 was built in 1891 and 1892, at a cost of $15,000. The impressive brick and stone building, an excellent example of Richardsonian Romanesque architecture, was Columbus' first engine house in a primarily residential area. It was designed to house a crew of eight men, four horses, a steam engine, and a hose wagon. As part of the German Village Historic District, it was placed on the National Register in 1974.

Proximity to three other stations decreed that No.5 be vacated in 1968; modern equipment could reach fires more quickly. The building was in good condition, but was threatened with demolition when restaurateur Chuck Muer purchased and adapted it as a restaurant.

The main dining room, in the area where engine and hose-wagon were stored, has a high pressed-tin ceiling and a brass fire pole. Wide doors are filled in with deep bays and large tables; other seating is divided by curtained booths into alcoves.

In the tower and bar, antique fire-fighting equipment and hoses create hanging sculptures, and smaller dining rooms, in stable and hayloft, are decorated with prints of famous fires.

"The Spot" basement tavern, named for dalmatian dogs, traditional firehouse mascots, has fire nets on its arched ceiling and a slate floor. The Spot's own menu includes many dishes cooked at tableside.

Chuck Muer's restaurants— there are thirty-three, of which four are in historic buildings— are known for fine seafood, and Engine House No.5 has some of the best. "We have an absolute commitment to quality and freshness," general manager Greg Keifer said. "Lobster and fish are flown in from Maine, Florida, and the Great Lakes, and all sauces are made here and assembled to order."

You may begin with gazpacho, spicy Charley's Chowder, or a dozen fresh seafood appetizers, and continue with grilled, poached, broiled, or blackened fish, depending upon what is fresh. There are pastas, chicken, and steak for diehards, and plenty of desserts. If you're celebrating, your cake will be delivered via the firepole, complete with blazing sparkler.

Engine House No.5, 121 Thurman Avenue, Columbus, Ohio 43206, is open for lunch Monday through Friday, 11:30 a.m. to 2:30 p.m., and for dinner Sunday through Thursday, 5 to 10 p.m., Friday and Saturday until 11 p.m. "The Spot" is open Tuesday through Saturday, 5 to 11 p.m. (614)443-4877. Dress is casual (tank tops and shorts prohibited), all legal beverages are served, including Sunday, and reservations are recommended to avoid a lengthy wait on weekends. Children's menu is available, and hostess should be alerted if visit is to celebrate an occasion. AE, CB, DC, MC, V, Discovery. ($$$)

ENGINE HOUSE NO.5 CHARLEY'S CHOWDER

¼ cup olive oil
3 medium cloves garlic, crushed
⅓ cup chopped onion
Pinch of oregano
Pinch of basil
Pinch of thyme
¾ cup chopped celery

6 ounces stewed tomatoes
3 quarts clam juice
1 pound boneless pollack or turbot
5 Tablespoons finely chopped parsley
Salt

In large pot, heat olive oil until very hot. Add garlic and cook until golden, then add onion and cook 1 to 2 minutes. Add spices and cook another minute, then add celery and cook until translucent. Add tomatoes, and cook 20 to 25 minutes, stirring frequently. Add clam juice and fish, and cook over high heat 15 minutes. Lower heat, cover pot, and continue cooking for 20 minutes. Stir frequently with wire whip to break up fish and blend flavors. To serve, sprinkle with parsley. Serves 6.

ENGINE HOUSE NO.5 ROLLS

2 ½ cups warm water
2 ½ ounces yeast (by weight)
2 heaping Tablespoons sugar

Pinch of salt
5 Tablespoons vegetable oil
2 ½ pounds high gluten flour

In large bowl, mix first 5 ingredients and allow to stand until yeast dissolves. Add flour and mix well for 5 minutes, or knead by hand until smooth. Divide dough into 4 portions, and, on floured surface, roll each to a tube about 25 inches long. Roll each loaf in 1 ounce of topping (see below) and place on well-greased baking sheet. With scissors, make 6 diagonal cuts almost through each loaf. Brush each loaf with garlic mixture (see below), brushing in the cuts as well. Bake at 450 degrees for 10 minutes. Makes 4 long loaves.

For topping: blend 3 ounces Kosher salt with 1 ounce poppy seeds.

For garlic mixture: in blender, blend 2 garlic cloves, crushed, with 3 ounces olive oil, 1 teaspoon basil, and 1 teaspoon oregano.

SCHMIDT'S SAUSAGE HAUS
Columbus

Columbus is a town built for a purpose: it was to be the capital of Ohio. There was already a settlement at the junction of the Scioto and Olentangy rivers called "Franklinton," on the site of an earlier Indian Village, but a new town was laid out on the east bank of the Scioto, and the Capitol was constructed in the wilderness in 1816.

The building was rapidly outgrown, and a grand new Capitol was finished in 1856. By then, Columbus had developed as an industrial and marketing force, as well as a center of government, and was the state's second largest city.

German immigrants clustered on the south side of Columbus. Hardworking brewers, carpenters, masons, and storekeepers, they built narrow red-brick houses close to the street in the German style, and established German churches and social organizations. The German Village, 233 acres of privately owned homes and businesses, was placed on the National Register in 1974.

In 1886, in the German community, J. Fred Schmidt started a packing company that eventually had distribution throughout Ohio. His son, George L., first cooked and sold Schmidt products at the Ohio State Fair in 1915, establishing a tradition that still holds. HIS sons, George F. and Grover, furthered retail sales by opening a store and restaurant in 1967, in the company's former livery stable.

Schmidt's Sausage Haus was intended to be a delicatessen with a few tables, but customers wanted more. The two-story brick stable, built in the 1890s, had a comfortable, relaxed atmosphere, with its brick walls, huge sliding wood doors, and simple foods. Hungry people waited in line for Schmidt's famous "Bahama Mama" sausage, hearty soups and chili, German specialties, and gooey desserts. Additional rooms were opened, the second floor was converted to banquet rooms, and oompah and jazz bands were brought in to entertain.

An upstairs fire in 1983 damaged the building, but business continued in a tent; the building was swiftly repaired, and there are now three other Schmidt's Sausage Haus locations, keeping the fourth generation of the family busy.

There's a reason for Schmidt's success: "We're conscious about quality," Geoff Schmidt, President, said. "We pay strict attention to it. Bread and beer are the only things we don't make here."

In addition to the Bahama Mama, Schmidt's sandwiches include their own bratwurst, in casing or patty style, and savory alternatives such as corned beef, boneless chicken breast, and reuben. Half-pound hamburgers, homemade soups and salads, and "Main Events" of sauerbraten, chicken and noodles, and Bavarian cabbage rolls come with a choice of excellent side dishes: German potato salad, red cabbage, and potato pancakes are just a few.

Desserts, all homemade, and all but one (a chocolate cream puff you won't believe!) on the menu since 1967, might make a meal in themselves, or may be selected from a case for carryout. Apple or peach strudel, German chocolate cake, coconut, banana, and chocolate cream pies are all tempting, but the Jumbo Cream Puff —flaky pastry the size of a softball, filled with pudding-y cream and dusted with powdered sugar— is the handsdown favorite of Schmidt's regulars.

Schmidt's Sausage Haus, 240 E. Kossuth Street, Columbus, Ohio 43206, is open 7 days a week, with continuous service. Monday hours are 11 a.m. to 9 p.m., Tuesday through Thursday until 12 Midnight, Friday and Saturday until 1 a.m. Sunday hours are 12 Noon to 10 p.m. In winter, Monday closing is 8 p.m. (614)444-6808. Dress is casual, but "muscle" shirts and bare feet are prohibited. All legal beverages are served, except Sunday, reservations are not accepted, and a children's menu is available. AE, MC, V. ($)

SCHMIDT'S SAUSAGE HAUS SWEET KRAUT

8 ounces sauerkraut	2 ounces onion, diced
3 ounces celery, diced	1 ounce salad oil
1 ounce green pepper, diced	1 ounce cider vinegar
	2 ½ ounces sugar

In large bowl, mix all ingredients well. Yields 18 ounces, at least 6 servings.

SCHMIDT'S SAUSAGE HAUS CHEESE TARTS

Six 4-ounce baked tart
  shells
8 ounces cream cheese
11 ounces sweetened
  condensed milk

3 ounces reconstituted
  lemon juice
1 teaspoon white vanilla
24 fresh cherries

In mixer bowl, whip cream cheese with half the condensed milk until smooth. Add remaining ingredients, and mix at low speed until well blended. Divide into pastry shells, and top each with 4 fresh cherries. Serves 6.

THE REFECTORY
Columbus

People in the wilderness, hungry for companionship and eager for salvation, flocked to religious meetings held by itinerant preachers. These gatherings often lasted for days, and started a religious revival that swept the country.

The Methodists visited the frontier as early as 1798, and provided circuit riders for congregations that could not afford a minister. In remote areas, services combined sermons, weddings, and baptisms, and helped to unify communities.

The lives of circuit riders were difficult and brief; they traveled on horseback over rude trails in all weathers. Despite exposure, malnutrition, and loneliness, the system lasted into the twentieth century.

Northwest of Columbus, a Methodist congregation shared a circuit rider with eight other churches, meeting in members' homes until 1854, when The Bethel Methodist Church was constructed. Standing timber was donated for the building, but volunteer laborers cut the wrong trees, and the church was built of black walnut the owner had hoped to sell.

In 1877, the railroad passed near the church. Noisy trains often halted services, so when the Perry Township schoolhouse came on the market in 1918, the church building was moved to share its grove of maples. The school was used for Sunday School, and in the 1950s, the two buildings were connected by a frame corridor that housed the church's first restrooms. Growth continued, and a new building was constructed further west on Bethel Road in 1977.

Called "The Refectory," the name for a dining hall in a religious house or college, the church/school became a restaurant in 1981, and is known for Continental-style cuisine and an awardwinning wine cellar. "We want to challenge ourselves to set the standards," said Kamal Boulos, general manager. "We aspire to evolve into one of the finest dining places in the area."

Luncheon might consist of Breast of Duckling Salad, with raspberry vinaigrette and fresh vegetables, or lamb chops grilled with herbed garlic butter— or a sampling of extraordinary appetizers: salmon gravlax with dill mayonnaise and baby vegetables, or shrimp with grapefruit and Louis sauce.

Dinner specialties include Sweetbreads with Morels, Quail Veronique, and Paupiettes of Dover Sole stuffed with lobster mousse; salads are fresh and delicious, and among dessert selections are outstanding pastries and a cloudlike white chocolate mousse.

The Refectory, 1092 Bethel Road, Columbus, Ohio 43220, is open for lunch 11:30 a.m. to 2 p.m. Monday through Friday, for Dinner 5:30 to 10 p.m. Monday through Thursday, to 11 p.m. Friday and Saturday. (614)451-9774. Most men wear jackets and ties, all legal beverages are served, and there is an extensive wine list and a Cruvinet system, providing many fine wines by the glass. Reservations are suggested and "really advisable," especially for 5 or more. AE, CB, DC, MC, V. ($$$)

THE REFECTORY CHICKEN WELLINGTON

Four 6-ounce chicken breasts, boned and skinned
Salt and pepper
3 ounces butter
1 shallot, minced
1 pound mushrooms, chopped fine
½ cup dry white wine
4 six-inch squares puff paste
2 Tablespoons butter
3 Tablespoons flour
1 cup chicken broth
¼ cup heavy cream

Season chicken breasts and sear in 3 ounces butter, browning on both sides. Cool. Sauté shallots and mushrooms in white wine; cook until dry, and cool. Place ¼ of this mixture on each piece of puff paste, top with a chicken breast, and enclose by folding corners together and sealing edges. Place on cookie sheet, sealed edges down, and bake at 400 degrees for 35 minutes. Blend remaining butter and flour in saucepan; add chicken broth, stirring constantly until thickened. Simmer 10 minutes, add cream, season with salt and pepper, and simmer five minutes more. Serve in sauceboat with chicken. Serves 4.

THE REFECTORY VEAL DIJONAISE

8 three-ounce veal
  scallops, pounded thin
Salt and pepper
Flour for dredging
4 ounces butter
2 ounces dry white wine

1 cup heavy cream
1 Tablespoon whole grain
  mustard
1 teaspoon Dijon mustard
6 artichoke hearts,
  quartered

Season veal, dredge in flour, and saute in butter, in batches if necessary. Remove veal to heated platter. Drain excess butter and deglaze skillet with wine, scraping bottom. Reduce wine to half, add cream, and simmer until reduced to desired consistency. Stir in mustards, heat artichoke hearts in sauce, check seasoning, and spoon over the veal. Serves 4.

THE REFECTORY CARAMEL CREAM
WITH ORANGES

Caramel (see below)
½ cup + 2 Tablespoons
  sugar
4 ¼ cups milk
1 vanilla bean OR 1
  teaspoon vanilla

Grated rind of one orange
¼ cup Curaçao or other
  orange-flavored liqueur
6 eggs + 2 yolks, beaten
Segments from one orange

In saucepan, dissolve sugar in milk, heat, add vanilla bean, grated orange rind, and Curaçao. Bring to boil, remove from heat, and let steep five minutes. Remove bean. Pour milk into eggs and stir. Strain mixture into caramel-lined molds. Place orange segments into molds, place molds in water bath, and bake one hour (or until set) at 325 degrees. Cool and serve. Tastes better if served the following day. Serves 6.

For caramel: Bring ¼ cup water and ¼ cup sugar to boil and cook to an amber color. Pour into six molds, tilting to coat sides and bottom.

THE WORTHINGTON INN
Worthington

The frontier would never have opened without the ambition and courage of men like James Kilbourne: on his own from the age of fifteen, he had become an Episcopal minister and achieved business success by the time he reached thirty.

After the American Revolution, New Englanders looked westward for new opportunity; in 1802, Reverend Kilbourne and Nathaniel Little were sent to explore Ohio by the Scioto Land Company of Granby, Connecticut.

When they returned, 16,000 acres of land was purchased for $20,000. A town was platted on paper, with provision for church, schools, and a village green, and in the spring of 1803, Kilbourne and others went to clear land, dig a well, and build temporary shelters. Settlers arrived in October, and the town was named for Thomas Worthington, later Governor of Ohio.

Worthington's location on the highway between the Ohio River and Lake Erie encouraged growth, until it lost— by one vote— the capital of Ohio in 1812.

Travelers often stopped at Worthington's Central House, built by Kilbourne's son-in-law, Rensselaer W. Cowles, in the early 1830s. The two-story, Federal style brick building was purchased for $5,000 in 1852 by Theodore Fuller, who added a south wing. Known briefly as the Union Hotel, then Hotel Central, it stayed primarily in the hands of one family until 1937.

A fire destroyed portions of the second floor and roof about 1900, and a third floor ballroom under a stylish Mansard roof and front porches were added when repairs were made. The building acquired the name "The Worthington Inn" in 1952, and was renovated and enlarged in 1983 by present owners, Epicurean Inns, Inc. With most of original Worthington, the inn was placed on the National Register in 1980.

Worthington Inn's three dining rooms and twenty-six overnight rooms, including five suites, are decorated with appropriate nineteenth-century antiques, with fine stenciling and wallpapers carrying out a scheme of rose, maroon, and blue-green.

Under the direction of Chef Keith Rinaldi, the inn's cuisine reflects the best of the country's bounty. Luncheon soups— French Onion and Pistou are favorites— and special sandwiches join fruit, chicken, seafood, and roquefort/bacon salads; entrées of chicken, veal, beef, and seafood, accompanied by fresh vegetable and potato, vie for your attention with pasta dishes, including Salmon Fettuccine.

At dinner, a full page of appetizers heads a list of soups and tempting salads (tomato and Mozzarella with greens and pesto), with entrées such as veal saltimbocca, sautéed breast of duckling with black truffle sauce, and charbroiled lamb chops.

Dessert choices at both meals are special: delicate creme brulée, mocha cheesecake, homemade gelato, and rich Belgian truffle torte.

The Worthington Inn, 649 North High Street, Worthington, Ohio 43085, is entered from the New England Street side, and is open for lunch Monday through Saturday, 11 a.m. to 3 p.m.; for dinner Monday through Thursday 5:30 to 10 p.m., Friday and Saturday until 11 p.m. Sunday lunch is 11 a.m. to 3 p.m., dinner 5:30 to 10 p.m. (614)885-7700. Daytime dress is casual; people dress more in the evening. All beverages are served, including Sunday, and there is an extensive wine list and 2 Cruvinet systems, providing many fine wines by the glass. Reservations are suggested, especially during September and for groups of 8 or more, and for overnight. AE, DC, MC, V. ($$$)

WORTHINGTON INN BAKED ARTICHOKES

3 marinated artichoke hearts, quartered
One ounce+ slice mozzarella cheese

One ounce+ slice baby Swiss cheese
½ ounce Romano cheese, grated

Warm artichoke hearts. Place on ovenproof serving dish, top with slices of cheese and sprinkle with Romano. Broil until bubbly. One serving.

WORTHINGTON INN BRIE AND ROASTED RED PEPPER SOUP

¼ pound butter
1 ½ cups flour
½ cup chopped celery
½ cup chopped onion

1 quart clam juice
1 pound Brie cheese and rind, chopped

3 sweet red peppers,   Salt and pepper
   roasted (see below) and
   pureed

In saucepan, blend butter and flour and cook over medium heat; add celery and onion and simmer 3 minutes. In large saucepan, heat clam juice to boiling. Whisk in butter mixture and stir until thickened. Stir in Brie until completely blended; strain into another pan. Add puréed peppers and correct seasoning. Serves 12.

To roast peppers, core, quarter, and roast under broiler until blackened. Place immediately in plastic bag until cool; remove skins under cold running water.

WORTHINGTON INN SCAMPI

4 large Gulf shrimp, peeled   1 ounce white wine
   and deveined   Pinch chopped fresh
2 Tablespoons butter   parsley
1 clove garlic, minced   Salt and pepper
1 small shallot, minced

In skillet, sauté shrimp, garlic, and shallot in butter one minute over medium high heat, turning shrimp once. Deglaze pan with wine, and season to taste. One serving.

WORTHINGTON INN RASPBERRY AND
WALNUT SALAD

3 or 4 leaves Bibb lettuce
4 medium leaves spinach
12 raspberries
3 Tablespoons chopped
   walnuts
Dressing (see below)

Arrange lettuce and spinach on plate, top with raspberries, and sprinkle with walnuts. Pour dressing over. One serving.

For dressing: slowly beat 1 cup walnut oil into ¼ cup raspberry vinegar. Season with salt and pepper.

101

BUN'S RESTAURANT AND BAKERY
Delaware

Delaware Indians, who moved westward into Ohio about 1700, found mineral springs in the Olentangy River valley. These attracted white settlers who named their village, and later their county, for the Indians. In the 1830s, when "taking the waters" was believed to have benefits, a large resort was built. It was not successful, and in 1842, the Ohio Methodists bought the property and turned it into Ohio Wesleyan University.

In that same year, George Frederick Hoffman, a Bavarian baker, immigrated to the United States. After serving in the Union Army, he settled in Delaware and opened a bakery in 1863. His son, George Julius Hoffman, moved the business to 10 Winter Street, and added a soda fountain.

HIS son, another George, nicknamed "Bun," with his brother Roy in charge of the bakery, gradually expanded the business into a restaurant, and opened two dining rooms in the 1920s. It was during this period that the restaurant acquired its name.

George Gabriel ("Biscuit") and his son George Michael eventually succeeded to the business, and operate the restaurant with #2 son, Steve. Mike's young son, George Christopher, occasionally "helps" in the bakery.

Five generations of the Hoffman family have made Delaware's second-oldest family business successful, providing quality food and service at a moderate price. The building they occupy was placed on the National Register in 1982, as part of the Sandusky Street Historic District.

A transitional Early Victorian commercial building, the two-story red brick structure has a central pediment and continuous stone lintels, which carry over to the second story of the three-story building next door. Half of this building was remodeled into an additional dining room for Bun's in 1969.

Guests enter through the bakery, surrounded by fragrant breads, buns, and rolls guaranteed to create an appetite. Breakfast specials are as traditional as Eggs BUNadict with crisp-fried potatoes, or as fanciful as corn tortillas with scrambled eggs and green chilies topped with cheese; lunch might be a sandwich on homemade bread or bun with homemade soup, an old fashioned plate lunch, or just homecooked vegetables with rolls and dessert.

103

Evening and Sunday dinners are strictly traditional: Steaks, fried scallops, roast beef or turkey with dressing, baked ham or creamed chicken in a patty shell. A wide selection of vegetables and salads are included, with homemade hot rolls.

Homemade ice creams, gooey fudge cake with chocolate icing, strawberry shortcake, and pies from the bakery are featured for dessert. Try lemon meringue, pecan, cinnamon apple, or blueberry, and if you don't have room left to eat a slice, buy a whole one and take it home—your family will love you!

Bun's Restaurant and Bakery, 6 West Winter Street, Delaware, Ohio 43015, is open Tuesday through Saturday, 7 a.m. to 8 p.m., and Sunday 11 a.m. to 8 p.m. Bakery opens at 10 a.m. on Sunday. (614)363-3731. Dress is casual, all legal beverages are served, including Sunday, and reservations are accepted, preferred for parties of 6 or more and on Sundays. Children's menu is available. MC, V, personal checks. ($$)

BUN'S HAM LOAF

2 Tablespoons minced
  onion
¾ cup bread crumbs
1 large egg

¼ cup milk
1 ¼ pounds ground ham
Salt and pepper
Brown sugar

In large bowl, combine first four ingredients, then mix in ham, salt, and pepper. Mold into a loaf, and cover loaf with brown sugar. Place in standard loaf pan and cover with foil. Bake at 325 degrees 1 ¾ to 2 hours, removing foil for last 20 minutes. Serves 5 or 6.

BUN'S FRUIT BARS

1 cup sugar
½ cup shortening
1 egg
¼ cup milk
¼ cup molasses
1 ½ teaspoons baking soda
1 ½ teaspoons salt
1 teaspoon cinnamon

Dash of nutmeg
⅛ teaspoon allspice
⅛ teaspoon cloves
⅛ teaspoon ginger
3 ¼ cups flour
10 ounces raisins
White icing (see below)

Cream sugar and shortening. Add egg, milk, and molasses and blend thoroughly. Stir in dry ingredients, then raisins. Roll dough ¼-inch thick, into strips the length of a cookie sheet and 3 inches wide. Place strips on greased cookie sheet and bake at 350 degrees 12 to 15 minutes. While hot, brush top lightly with milk. Cool, then ice with frosting made of confectioners' sugar mixed with a little vanilla and just enough milk to spread. Cut into bars about an inch wide. Yields about 4 dozen bars.

BUN'S BUTTERSCOTCH MUFFINS

1 cup sugar
3 teaspoons salt
1 ½ cups shortening
Eggs to yield 1 ¼ cups (7 or 8)
3 cups water

8 cups cake flour
¾ cup powdered milk
5 Tablespoons baking powder
10 ounces butterscotch bits

In large bowl, cream sugar, salt, and shortening. Add eggs, then water, and mix in dry ingredients just until moistened. Quickly blend in butterscotch bits. Divide into greased muffin tins and bake at 400 degrees until lightly browned. Yields 3 dozen large muffins.

BIDDIE'S COACH HOUSE
Dublin

When Franklin County was formed in 1803, there were already settlers in what would become Dublin, Ohio; Ludwick Sells and his family from Huntingdon County, Pennsylvania, had arrived in April, 1800.

After the War of 1812, some of the Sells family wanted to invest in land in the area, but had insufficient funds. John Sells, a brother who had settled in Augusta, Kentucky, was convinced to put up most of the money, and it is he who is considered the town's founder.

When John Shields, surveyor and friend of John Sells, surveyed the land and divided it into lots, he said, "You must name it for Dublin, Ireland, my home town, which it resembles."

By 1818, the name was in use in a quaint little town of stone and log houses nestled on the banks of the Scioto. Techniques of construction observed in Pennsylvania and Kentucky were used for the vernacular Federal style houses.

A small frame house on High Street was built in the early 1830s by Cornelius Ortman; a two-story section was added to the north by Holcomb Tuller about 1850. It was a stagecoach inn on the Granville-Greenville route, but when Cicero Sells and his wife, Mary Johnson Sells, bought the property in 1898, it became The Sells Hotel. As part of the Washington Township Multiple Resource Area, it was placed on the National Register in 1979.

"Aunt" Mary Sells, who emigrated from Ireland in the late 1850s as a very young girl, had been a servant in the Sells household before marrying Cicero. A woman of remarkable character, she had a reputation as a good cook, and was responsible for the success of the hotel.

When Mary Marsalka, a former teacher, was looking for a location for a tearoom, the former hotel was used as an office; she bought it, restored it, and installed her charming mother, Elizabeth "Biddie" Renick as hostess. Once again, remarkable women are in charge in the building now called "Biddie's Coach House," and, once again, it is successful because of its food.

"My main premise," Mary said, "is that I don't serve anything I would not serve at home. We make everything here, fresh daily."

With added touches of hot muffins in a "Little Biddie Basket" and a tearoom atmosphere that men find perfectly comfortable, Biddie's offers the best luncheon you're likely to find. Hot soups— a buttery, rich cream of broccoli is superb— plus chilled ones in summer, set off "Mr. Biddie's Sandwich" of roast beef in a sharp sauce, chicken or spinach salad, or a daily special seafood, such as salmon mousse with dill sauce.

And desserts? You'll have a hard time choosing between dense crème caramel with whipped cream and toasted almonds, tart lemon pie with thick meringue, warm apple cake with cinnamon sauce, and the signature "Flower Pot Dessert": chocolate cake and ice cream with Belgian chocolate sauce and whipped cream.

Biddie's Coach House, 76 South High Street, Dublin, Ohio 43017, is open for lunch only, 11 a.m. to 2:30 p.m. Monday through Saturday. It is available for private parties in the evening. (614)764-9359. Attire is "Dressy casual," alcoholic beverages are not served, and reservations are accepted, especially in summer. No credit cards are accepted. ($$)

BIDDIE'S LEMON BREAD

½ cup butter	1 teaspoon baking powder
1 cup sugar	½ teaspoon salt
2 eggs	½ cup chopped pecans
Rind of one lemon, grated	½ cup milk
1 ¾ cups flour	Lemon glaze (see below)

Cream butter and sugar, beat in eggs thoroughly. Add remaining ingredients, mixing until well blended. Divide batter into 2 greased 8" x 4" loaf pans and bake at 350 degrees until brown and firm, about 45 minutes. Spoon glaze over hot bread while in pans. Freezes nicely.

For lemon glaze: blend juice of 1 lemon with ½ cup sugar until sugar is dissolved.

BIDDIE'S HERB CHEESE SOUFFLE

¾ cup margarine
¾ cup flour
3 cups milk
3 cups grated cheese
10 eggs, separated
1 teaspoon ground
  mustard

1 Tablespoon Dijon
  mustard
1 teaspoon salt
¼ teaspoon pepper
2 teaspoons tarragon
1 Tablespoon dry parsley
1 teaspoon marjoram

In saucepan over medium heat, melt margarine, add flour, and stir, while adding milk. Cook until thick; stir in cheese and remove from heat. Beat egg yolks until thick, adding herbs. Beat whites until stiff. Mix yolk mixture with cheese sauce; add a fourth of egg whites to lighten. Gently fold in rest of whites, turn into greased 9″ x 13″ pan and bake in hot water bath at 350 degrees until brown and firm, about 45 minutes. Makes twelve 3-inch squares.

BIDDIE'S GERMAN APPLE CAKE

1 cup oil
3 eggs
2 cups sugar
1 teaspoon vanilla
2 cups flour
1 teaspoon soda
½ teaspoon salt

2 teaspoons cinnamon
4 cups peeled, chopped
  apples
1 cup chopped pecans
Cream cheese topping (see
  below)

In large bowl, mix all ingredients. Pour into greased 9″ x 13″ pan, and bake at 350 degrees about 45 minutes.

For topping: blend 8 ounces cream cheese, at room temperature, with 3 Tablespoons butter, 1 teaspoon vanilla, and 1 ½ cups confectioners' sugar. Spread on warm cake.

THE RED BRICK TAVERN
Lafayette

The first tracks through the wilderness were made by buffalo, followed by Indians and explorers, then soldiers defending the frontier. When settlers began moving westward, it was obvious that improved roads were needed.

In 1802, the Enabling Act set aside funds for a road to Ohio, beginning at Cumberland, Maryland. States whose lands would be crossed did not approve a route until 1811, and further delay was caused by the War of 1812. Construction finally began in 1814, but Congress had made no provision for road repair or extension into Ohio.

The project was halted for a decade by fear that a road built and maintained by the federal government would lessen state sovereignty. In 1824, ground was at last broken at St. Clairsville; the road would connect Columbus, Indianapolis, and Vandalia, then capital of Illinois, a distance of nearly 600 miles.

The National Road not only facilitated western expansion, but improved communication and unified the country. Mail coaches sped back and forth, manufactured goods reached the west more quickly and at lower cost, and cattle and other western produce moved rapidly eastward on its crowded surface.

In 1837, Stanley Watson, newly arrived from Connecticut, built a handsome two-story brick tavern in the Federal style beside the brand-new National Road, halfway between Columbus and Springfield. John McMullen, innkeeper, ran the Red Brick Tavern until 1850.

Called "splendid" when it was completed, the tavern had twenty-four overnight rooms, which hosted six U.S. presidents and such notables as Henry Clay and P.T. Barnum.

Traffic on The National Road slowed with the coming of the railroads, and the Red Brick Tavern was used as a residence until the road was widened to become U.S. 40, when the tavern became a restaurant. It was placed on the National Register in 1975, and celebrates its sesquicentennial in 1987.

Operated since 1982 by Gene and Shirley Freet, The Red Brick Tavern maintains its nineteenth century atmosphere, although changes have been made. The former taproom, filled with interesting antiques, serves as lobby; the "ladies' parlor" is a cozy bar, and the airy main dining room, with oil lamps gleaming in tall shuttered windows, is pervaded with the delicious fragrance of hot cinnamon rolls.

The menu offers an extensive choice of well-prepared seafoods and steaks, plus pork and lamb chops, ham, veal, and chicken, served with choice of vegetable and salad, and, of course, cinnamon rolls and biscuits with apple butter. Wednesday is fried chicken night; Thursday offers seafood, with all the crab legs you can eat. A piano player takes requests on weekends, and there's a Dixieland band the last Tuesday of every month.

The Red Brick Tavern is on Route 40 at Lafayette, just off I-70. Mailing address is P.O. Box 14, London, Ohio 43140. Hours are 11 a.m. to 9 p.m. Monday through Thursday, to 10 p.m. Friday and Saturday, and to 7 p.m. Sunday, with continuous service. (614)852-1474. Dress is "comfortable," all legal beverages are served (except Sunday), and reservations are accepted, recommended on weekends or holidays, and preferred for parties of 5 or more. AE, DC, MC, V. ($$)

RED BRICK TAVERN SWEET POTATO PUFF

3 pounds cooked OR
  canned sweet potatoes
¾ teaspoon allspice
¾ teaspoon nutmeg
¾ teaspoon cinnamon
2 teaspoons vanilla
¾ teaspoon honey
¾ teaspoon margarine

½ cup brown sugar
2 eggs
2 ounces tiny
  marshmallows
Nuts and additional
  marshmallows to cover
  top

Drain potatoes, place in large mixer bowl, add other ingredients except nuts and additional marshmallows, and whip until smooth and fluffy. Spread in greased baking pan and sprinkle with nuts and marshmallows. Bake at 350 degrees for 30 minutes, or until brown and firm on top.

RED BRICK TAVERN PAN FRIED CHICKEN

Chicken, cut into serving
  pieces
1 egg
2 cups milk
Pinch of garlic salt

4 cups flour
⅛ cup salt, or to taste
⅛ cup pepper
⅛ cup garlic salt

Beat egg, milk, and garlic salt until well blended. Soak chicken in this mixture about five minutes. Mix dry ingredients, and use to bread soaked chicken. Pan fry chicken in peanut oil, turning frequently, for 45 minutes or until crisp.

RED BRICK TAVERN OLD FASHIONED
CINNAMON ROLLS

2 cakes yeast
¼ cup lukewarm water
¾ cup milk, scalded
1 ½ teaspoons salt
¼ cup sugar

½ cup shortening
About 5 cups flour
3 eggs, beaten
Margarine
Cinnamon

Dissolve yeast in water. Add salt, sugar, and shortening to milk and cool to lukewarm. Add 2 cups flour and mix well; blend in yeast and eggs, add remaining flour and mix to a soft dough. Turn out onto floured surface and knead until shiny. Place in greased container, cover, and let rise until doubled in size. Punch down, grease surface, cover and place in refrigerator until needed. Roll out portions of dough on floured surface to about ½ inch thick, spread with softened margarine and sprinkle with cinnamon. Roll dough up like jelly roll and cut into 1-inch slices. Place on greased baking sheet to rise, then bake at 400 degrees. Spread with margarine immediately, then with frosting made of confectioners' sugar mixed with a little vanilla and just enough milk to spread.

THE MILAN INN
Milan

Half a million acres of Connecticut's Western Reserve were set aside as the "Sufferer's Tract," or "Firelands," and were given to those who had been burned out by the British during the Revolution. Many towns and townships in present-day Erie and Huron counties are named for places in Connecticut.

A Moravian mission to the Indians, abandoned in 1809, provided the site for the village of Milan; Ebenezer Merry built a dam and a mill on the Huron River in 1816, and laid out the village in 1817. By 1824, there were 280 people and thirty-two houses, and residents had determined to build a canal to Lake Erie.

Milan (pronounced MY lan) included shops, a tavern, tanneries, several blacksmiths, tailors, cabinetmakers, wagoners, a saddler, a lawyer, and a doctor. Brick store buildings were constructed, and a hat factory, two "asheries," which made lye, and a plow factory provided employment. Two church congregations and a school attracted more people, and, in 1833, the town was incorporated.

The Milan Canal, opened in 1839, was a ships' canal, deeper and wider than barge canals; lake schooners were towed three miles from Huron to the canal basin, making Milan a port on Lake Erie. Fourteen warehouses stored goods awaiting shipment, and shipyards constructed additional ships— some seventy-five schooners were built in Milan between 1841 and 1868. Shipping had already been slowed by railroads when the 1869 flood destroyed the basin's dam, and it was never rebuilt.

Many structures from Milan's period of greatest prosperity remain, forming a quaint New England-style village around a square.

A fine example of a mid-nineteenth-century commercial building is the Milan Inn, built in 1845; its handsome bracketed front and elaborate window molds attest to its original cost. The western third of the building, housing the newspaper office of *The Milan Ledger,* was destroyed by an explosion in 1969, and was demolished, as may be seen by the off-center pediment. As part of the Milan Historic District, it was placed on The National Register in 1975.

The Inn's interior, damaged by fire in the 1890s and altered in the 1969 remodeling, is nevertheless interesting. Murals by local artist Martha Hutchinson depict events in Milan history, while memorabilia of Milan native Thomas A. Edison recall some of his inventions. Refurbished in 1986 by new owner (and Mayor of Milan) Robert Bickley, who has restored many of the area's historic buildings, The Milan Inn is once again "The Inn of Fine Foods" that it was in the 1960s, and Dorothy Kelley has returned as kitchen supervisor.

Aiming for leisured dining in a friendly atmosphere, the Milan Inn's waitresses, neat in maroon and white, present hot breads— cornsticks, rich sticky buns, and bran muffins— on a tray, and a choice of salads as well. Fruit juice appetizers and homemade soups precede mid-day sandwiches, luncheon salads, and entrees, while dinner entrées of steaks, ham, mixed grill, sweet and sour chicken, and seafoods are heartier. Offered at both meals, the fried perch in cracker meal is particularly crisp and delicious, and homemade pies with flaky crusts, such as apple with crumb topping, and creamy peanut butter meringue, are making a little Milan history themselves.

The Milan Inn, 29 East Church Street, Milan, Ohio 44846, is open Tuesday through Saturday, for lunch from 11 a.m. to 2:30 p.m., and for dinner from 5 to 9 p.m. Breakfast, Saturday and Sunday only, is from 7 to 11 a.m., and service is continuous until 9 p.m. Saturday and 8 p.m. Sunday. (419)499-4604. No alcoholic beverages are served, dress is casual, and reservations are accepted, preferred for larger groups. A children's menu and non-smoking areas are available. MC, V. ($$)

MILAN INN CORNSTICKS

1 cup flour
1 cup corn meal
¼ cup sugar
4 teaspoons baking powder
1 teaspoon salt

1 egg
½ teaspoon baking soda
1 ¼ cups buttermilk
¼ cup melted shortening or lard

Measure dry ingredients (except soda) into bowl and add egg. Mix soda with ¼ cup buttermilk and add, then beat in remaining milk, then shortening. Mix well, and pour into hot, greased cast-iron cornstick pan. Bake at 425 degrees for 18 minutes.

MILAN INN CHICKEN IN BARBECUE SAUCE

¾ cup chopped onion
1 cup + 1 Tablespoon sugar
1 ½ cups catsup
½ cup vinegar

3 teaspoons
Worcestershire sauce
1 ½ cups water

In saucepan, combine ingredients and simmer 1 ½ hours, until thickened. Place breaded, fried, chicken pieces in baking pan. Pour this sauce over chicken, and bake at 325 degrees for 45 minutes.

MILAN INN RUM SAUCE

1 cup brown sugar, packed
2 Tablespoons cornstarch
¼ teaspoon salt

2 cups boiling water
¼ cup butter
½ cup gold label rum

In saucepan, mix dry ingredients, and add boiling water gradually, stirring constantly. Bring to boil and simmer 5 minutes. Remove from heat and blend in butter and rum. Yields 2 cups; serve over mince pie or ice cream.

HOMESTEAD INN
Milan

Eighteen hundred and seventy people from Connecticut relocated to "The Firelands," bringing with them their New England customs and naming new towns for those destroyed by Tory raids during the Revolution. Industrious, ambitious people, these settlers rapidly turned the fertile soil of North Central Ohio into rich farmland.

Turnpikes, canals, and later, railroads bustled with loads of grain, produce, and stock to Lake Erie docks, and well-to-do farmers put up imposing residences in the midst of their acreage.

In 1883, Levi Arnold and his wife, Rachel, built a large two-story frame house on their strawberry farm outside Milan, incorporating elements of several popular styles. Its low-pitched, bracketed Italianate roof was topped with wrought-iron railing around a widow's walk, and tall windows admitted an unusual amount of light. According to legend, the farm was so prosperous that the house and its furnishings were paid for from the profits of only one year's crop.

After the completion of the Lake Shore Electric Railway in 1893, Arnold had a refrigerated rail car constructed for shipping his strawberries, which were loaded on his own rail siding, then taken to Norwalk or Sandusky. The house and strawberry farm remained in the Arnold family for three generations, and the house became a restaurant in the late 1950s, when the Ohio Turnpike passed nearby.

Owned and operated since 1979 by Mr. and Mrs. Robert Berry and Mr. and Mrs. Douglas Berry, the house is entered from the side, beneath a two-story portico added in an earlier remodeling. The interior, decorated attractively in the Victorian manner but incorporating pastel shades of rose and blue, is divided into several cozy dining rooms, with the basement rathskeller a European-flavored alternative, its massive stone walls and romantic recesses very popular with courting couples.

The Homestead Inn's food is American, "But not farm-type," said Doug Berry, manager and president. "We do a lot of sautéeing and broiling. We want people to feel they're getting their money's worth, but we do not sacrifice quality."

In that pursuit, they provide extensive choices at all times of day. Breakfasts range from hearty cattlemen's style to light omelets or potato shells filled with scrambled eggs and cheese; lunch might be a special sandwich or salad, or broiled chicken or beef kabob with rice. Snacks are available between meals, drawn from appetizers and sandwiches, and dinner menus offer steaks, chicken, veal, seafoods, and "Creative Cuisine" of the American Heart Association. An array of desserts, presented on a tray, is a final temptation: don't miss the streusel peach pie!

The Homestead Inn Restaurant, 12018 US 250, Milan, Ohio 44846, is visible from Gate 7 of the Ohio Turnpike, and is open from 7:15 a.m. to 9:30 p.m. Monday through Thursday, to 10 p.m. Friday and Saturday, and until 8:30 p.m. Sunday, with continuous service, although menus change during the day. (419)499-4271. Dress is casual, and all legal beverages are served, except Sunday. Reservations are accepted on weeknights, but only for parties of 6 or 8 on weekends. AE, DC, MC, V. ($$)

HOMESTEAD INN DEVILLED EGGS

12 hard-cooked eggs
½ teaspoon salt
¼ teaspoon pepper
3 Tablespoons sugar
1 teaspoon cider vinegar

1 Tablespoon prepared
  mustard
⅓ cup salad dressing or
  mayonnaise
Celery seed

Shell eggs; cut in half lengthwise and separate whites from yolks. Place yolks in a bowl and mash with a fork or pastry blender until fine crumbs. Add remaining ingredients, blend until smooth, then fill whites with yolk mixture. Use of a pastry bag is recommended. Sprinkle with celery seed.

HOMESTEAD INN SWEET POTATO BREAD

1 cup mashed yams
½ cup oil or shortening
⅓ cup water
1 ¾ cups flour
1 ½ cups sugar
½ cup chopped walnuts

1 teaspoon baking soda
1 teaspoon grated lemon
  rind
¾ teaspoon cinnamon
¾ teaspoon nutmeg
½ teaspoon salt

In large bowl, combine first 3 ingredients and beat well; add dry ingredients and beat well. Pour into greased bread pan and bake for about an hour at 350 degrees. Brush with glaze while still warm.

For glaze: blend 4 Tablespoons powdered sugar with 1 Tablespoon butter, add 1 Tablespoon milk and 1 Tablespoon lemon juice, and blend well.

HOMESTEAD INN BANANA PUDDING WITH WALNUT CRUST

For crust: blend ½ cup margarine, 1 cup flour, and 1 cup finely chopped walnuts. Press in bottom of 9″ x 13″ pan and bake at 350 degrees until light brown. Cool.

For first layer:

8 ounces cream cheese　　**10 ounces whipped**
1 cup powdered sugar　　　**topping**

Beat together and spread on prepared crust. Top with sliced bananas, then pudding layer.

For pudding layer:

3 egg yolks　　　　　　**2 cups milk**
1 cup sugar　　　　　　**Banana flavoring**
3 Tablespoons cornstarch

In saucepan, blend ingredients and cook over medium heat until thick. Cool before spreading over cream cheese and banana layer, then top with whipped topping or sweetened whipped cream. Refrigerate, and cut into 12 squares to serve.

BAXTER'S STONE HOUSE
Sandusky

Until Cleveland and Toledo were selected as terminal points on the Ohio Canal system, Sandusky was the premier port on Lake Erie. Grain wagons crowded the streets, and incoming ships brought new settlers.

Many newcomers were Germans who realized the grape-growing potential of the region; shipping gave way to fishing, vineyards, and breweries as the main local industries.

Ohio's first railroad, the Mad River and Lake Erie, was dedicated in Sandusky in 1835, but the town was also an important "station" on the underground railroad, by which escaping slaves were conducted to safety in Canada. Many fugitives were aided by a settlement of Black people who lived in Perkins Township as early as the 1830s, on what is now Perkins Avenue.

In 1863, Allen Remington purchased twelve acres of land near the former Black settlement. Stories are told that Remington and an uncle had built a stone house on the land years earlier, and made cider in an abandoned Black church. Remington operated a brick kiln and a fishing fleet, and is believed to have hidden runaway slaves in the stone house's cellar, before sailing them across the lake.

Although he died in 1911, and the property has been used for a variety of purposes since, the "The Stone House" has been an important landmark in Sandusky for generations.

It was a favorite restaurant of the Baxter family. In the 1970s, they purchased it, added a new kitchen, and enlarged the cellar into the "Underground Lounge." Presently run by James "Jimmy" Baxter, it retains much of its earlier flavor.

"We've tried to keep everything pretty much original," he said. "Some recipes have been with the Stone House for years: our hash browns, and the way we do perch and pickerel. Everything is cooked to order."

Under the direction of Chef Dan Boyer, The Stone House's food attracts an enormous following. The cozy gold and blue "Fireplace Room" and the "Porch Room," added in the 1950s, are crowded with people who appreciate excellent cooking in a relaxed atmosphere.

Salad lunches of shrimp, chicken, and a hearty house combination join omelets, sandwiches— perch is a favorite— and light entrees. At dinner, generous servings of perch and pick-erel head a list of seafoods, chicken, several veal choices, steaks and chops. All are served with appetizer, salad with homemade dressings, and potato— including the famous hash browns— plus hot rolls and delicious zucchini bread.

Save room for dessert: they're all treats, and the elderberry pie, in season, is warm and juicy, in a flaky crust. Like Baxter's Stone House, it is a taste of nostalgia.

Baxter's Stone House, 1338 Perkins Avenue, Sandusky, Ohio 44870, is 2 blocks east of U.S. 250, just off U.S. 6. It is open for lunch 11 a.m. to 2 p.m., Monday through Friday, for dinner 4:30 to 11 p.m. Monday through Saturday, and 12 Noon to 9 p.m. on Sunday. The Underground Lounge is open 3 p.m. to 2 a.m., 7 days a week. (419)626-4141. Dress is casual, and all legal beverages are served, including Sunday. Special prices prevail on a "Before Six" menu; children's menu is available. Reservations are advised. AE, DC, MC, V. ($$)

BAXTER'S STONE HOUSE CELERY SEED DRESSING

1 Tablespoon dry mustard	¾ cup sugar
2 teaspoons salt	1 ½ cups salad oil
2 teaspoons celery seed	3 ounces cider vinegar
1 ½ teaspoons paprika	3 ounces water

In bowl, blend all dry ingredients. Add liquids and blend thoroughly. Refrigerate. Yields about 3 cups.

BAXTER'S STONE HOUSE SEAFOOD MOZZARELLA

4 Tablespoons butter	¾ cup diced green peppers
3 cloves garlic, crushed	¾ cup fresh diced
8 ounces shelled raw	mushrooms
shrimp, cut up	½ cup diced onion
8 ounces scallops	4 to 6 slices mozzarella
8 ounces snow crab meat	cheese
1 cup white wine	

In large pot, melt butter, add garlic and seafoods, and sauté three minutes over medium heat. Add remaining ingredients except cheese, and sauté about 5 minutes. Spoon portions into deep individual serving dishes and top with cheese. Place in broiler or microwave 1 to 2 minutes to melt cheese. Serves 4 to 6.

BAXTER'S STONE HOUSE ZUCCHINI NUT BREAD

3 eggs
1 ½ teaspoons vanilla
2 cups sugar
1 cup salad oil
½ cups chopped pecans or walnuts
2 cups chopped zucchini, including skin

1 ½ teaspoons salt
1 Tablespoon cinnamon
1 ½ teaspoons baking soda
½ teaspoon baking powder
3 cups unsifted flour

In mixer, blend first 3 ingredients until fluffy, then add oil and mix 2 minutes. Add remaining ingredients and mix well. Pour into greased and floured 9" x 5" loaf pans, filling about ⅔ full, and bake at 325 degrees for about an hour, or until toothpick comes out clean. Yields 2 or 3 loaves.

BAXTER'S STONE HOUSE EASY CHOCOLATE MOUSSE

12 ounces Hershey's chocolate chip morsels
2 eggs
1 ½ cups scalding milk

1 teaspoon sugar
Pinch salt
Whipped cream for garnish

Place all ingredients in blender; let stand 1 minute. Blend at high speed 1 minute. Pour into 8 serving dishes; chill at least 2 hours. Top with whipped cream. Serves eight.

MON AMI RESTAURANT AND WINERY
Port Clinton

By the middle of the nineteenth century, the long growing season and loamy soil along the shores of Lake Erie had proven ideal for the culture of Catawba grapes. German immigrants brought old-world skills that produced distinguished wines, and numerous wineries were founded.

In 1872, the Neal and Ellithorp families established the Catawba Wine Company, constructing a huge two-and-a-half-story building of limestone quarried on the site. A growers' cooperative supplied grapes, and the winery's vaulted cellars provided storage for 130,000 gallons of wine and champagne.

The area still produces wine, but is now known more as a fishing and boating resort, and Mon Ami Winery, owned by Meiers since 1980, is one of only four wineries remaining in Ottawa county.

After a 1943 fire destroyed the interior, part of the building became a restaurant, operated since 1980 by Nathan Buckantz, who restored the building. It was placed on the National Register in 1983.

"I've created a gourmet restaurant with moderate prices in a resort area," he said. "We serve a thousand people a day in the summer— I know I'm on the right track."

A meal at Mon Ami might include Lake Erie perch or pickerel, or a fresh seafood specialty, with potato, salad, and crunchy rolls. At lunch, there are salads, cold plates, and hearty sandwiches; dinner adds prime rib, pastas, and duckling, and both meals end with a cart of homemade pastries— fluffy Amaretto pie in a flaky crust, or rich Kahlúa and Cream.

And the winery provides sparkling and still wines to accompany meals, and to take home as souvenirs of a pleasant visit.

Mon Ami Restaurant and Historic Winery, 3845 East Wine Cellar Road, Port Clinton, Ohio 43452, is open from 11:30 a.m. to 10 p.m., seven days a week; lounge is open until 2:30 a.m. during the summer. (419)797-4445. Dress is casual, reservations are not accepted in June, July, and August, and entertainment is provided on weekends, year round. All legal beverages and Mon Ami wines are available; there is a children's menu. AE, MC, V. ($$$)

127

MON AMI WINE SOUP

5 egg yolks
2 Tablespoons sugar
2 Tablespoons cornstarch
1 cup water
2 cups Mon Ami dry
   Catawba wine

1 teaspoon grated lemon
   peel
2 cloves

In mixing bowl, beat yolks with sugar, cornstarch, and water. Pour into top of double boiler. Add remaining ingredients, and whisk over boiling water until soup boils, about three minutes. Serves 6.

MON AMI DRESSING FOR SPINACH SALAD

⅓ cup tomato juice
2 Tablespoons salad oil
1 teaspoon salt
3 Tablespoons vinegar

¾ teaspoon dry mustard
1 teaspoon grated onion

Place all ingredients in a jar and shake well. Yields ¾ cup; may be made ahead and stored in refrigerator.

SCALLOPS À LA MON AMI

1 ½ pounds scallops
Juice of ½ lemon
¼ teaspoon salt
¼ teaspoon white pepper
½ cup flour
6 Tablespoons (approx.)
   vegetable oil
3 shallots, peeled and
   minced

3 cloves garlic, minced
¼ teaspoon dried basil
2 Tablespoons butter
1 Tablespoon chopped
   parsley
½ cup Mon Ami dry
   Catawba wine
¼ teaspoon
   Worcestershire sauce

Rinse scallops and pat dry. Sprinkle with lemon juice and season. Place in strainer, sprinkle with flour, and shake off excess. In heavy skillet, heat 3 Tablespoons oil, add scallops and toss over medium heat about 5 to 7 minutes, adding more oil if needed. Add shallots, garlic, and basil, and cook

3 minutes more. Remove from heat; stir in butter, parsley, wine, and Worcestershire. Serve immediately over rice.

MON AMI OREO COOKIE CHEESECAKE

For crust: mix 1 ¼ cups Oreo cookie crumbs with ¼ cup melted butter; press in bottom of 9″ springform pan and refrigerate ½ hour.

For filling:

2 pounds cream cheese, at room temperature
1 ½ cups sugar, divided
2 Tablespoons flour
4 extra-large eggs
2 large egg yolks
⅓ cup whipping cream
2 teaspoons vanilla, divided
1 ½ cups Oreo cookie crumbs
2 cups sour cream

In large mixer bowl, beat cream cheese until fluffy. Add 1 ¼ cups sugar and flour, then blend in eggs and yolks until smooth. Stir in cream and 1 teaspoon vanilla. Pour half this mixture into prepared pan, sprinkle with crumbs, and pour in remaining batter. Bake 15 minutes at 425 degrees; reduce temperature to 225 degrees and bake 50 minutes. Cover loosely with foil if browning too quickly. Increase temperature to 350 degrees; blend sour cream, ¼ cup sugar, and 1 teaspoon vanilla. Spread over cheesecake and bake 7 minutes. Refrigerate overnight. Top with glaze (see below) and garnish.

For glaze: combine 1 cup scalded whipping cream with 8 ounces semi-sweet chocolate and 1 teaspoon vanilla, and stir 1 minute. Refrigerate 15 minutes before pouring over chilled cheesecake.

Note: recipes courtesy Bonnie Van Gorder, who is preparing a Mon Ami cookbook.

THE ISLAND HOUSE
Port Clinton

Oliver Hazard Perry was only twenty-seven years old in 1813, when he accepted command of the Lake Erie campaign. The United States had no navy in the West; due to Niagara Falls, Lake Erie was inaccessible to ships on Lake Ontario, and there were few shipbuilders on the lake.

In only six months, Perry constructed, armed, and manned a squadron of one brig, six schooners, and one sloop, with which he defeated the British in a three-hour battle that hastened the end of the war.

The day of the battle was calm, but lake storms are sudden and violent, often lasting two days and nights. Such was the case in 1825, when would-be settlers bound for Illinois were shipwrecked in a natural harbor near the mouth of the Portage River.

Rather than continue their voyage, they decided to stay on the spot, and named their town "Port Clinton," for New York Governor De Witt Clinton.

After railroads made travel easier, the shores of Lake Erie swarmed with tourists, and by the 1880s and 1890s, excursion trains brought visitors from Cincinnati and the South.

In 1886, Conrad Gernhard built a three-story red brick hotel at the intersection of Madison and Perry streets in Port Clinton. Incorporating elements of several Victorian architectural styles, and sporting a cupola tower on the corner, the hotel was operated by Gernhard's son, Frank, until 1921. In a hundred years, there have been only four owners of the Island House, which was purchased and extensively renovated in 1986.

Over the years, the building has been altered and enlarged numerous times; the most recent changes utilized beaded oak wainscots and woodwork and Victorian reproduction light fixtures to evoke the period of the hotel's construction. The original entrance at the corner is now the Grill Room, but the bar, with its magnificent pressed-tin ceiling and original back bar, was always the bar. Tweedy blue-gray wallpaper enhances the overall effect of light and subdued comfort, a relaxing change from the sunny outdoors.

Chef John Wrobbel believes in using fresh local produce

and meats, with hearty sauces. "I like to cook within Ohio," he said, "what we're noted for in the Midwest."

One thing the lake region is known for is fish, and you'll find some of the best at The Island House. Pickerel and perch are offered in several preparations and combinations, both as appetizers and entrées. Other choices include steaks, veal, poultry and pork in the large portions that are a specialty.

Of course there are burgers and sandwiches at lunch, as well as enormous salads and light entrées, and the "Knife and Fork Soups" that are truly a meal in themselves.

Desserts change daily, but home-baked pies and fresh fruit cobblers are especially good in summer, and there's also persimmon cake and bread pudding with dried fruit, topped with bourbon whipped cream.

The Island House Inn, 102 Madison Street, Port Clinton, Ohio 43452, has seasonal hours. In summer, breakfast is served 7 to 11 a.m., lunch 11 a.m. to 2 p.m., and dinner 5 to 10 p.m. weeknights, to 11 p.m. Friday and Saturday. There are 37 rooms available for overnight stays. (419)734-2166. Dress is casual, all legal beverages are served, including Sunday, no reservations are accepted in summer, but are preferred for parties of 10 or more. There are 3 dining rooms and a coffee shop, with a wide range of prices. Children's menu is available. AE, CB, DC, MC, V. ($ to $$$)

ISLAND HOUSE BREAD PUDDING

¼ pound raisins	1 teaspoon lemon extract
8 eggs	About 2 loaves bread,
1 cup + 1 Tablespoon sugar	cubed
Pinch of salt	¼ cup dried peaches
1 quart milk, scalded	¼ cup dried prunes
2 teaspoons vanilla	

In bowl, soak raisins in hot water to cover. In large bowl, combine eggs, sugar, and salt. Add cooled milk, then flavorings, and set aside. Drain raisins and set aside. Grease large, shallow, ovenproof pan; layer bread cubes with raisins, peaches, and prunes, beginning with bread. Pour milk mixture evenly over bread, sprinkle with streusel topping (see below) and place pan in slightly larger pan half filled with water. Bake at 375 degrees until center is firm; allow to stand 15 minutes before serving. Top with whipped cream flavored with bourbon whiskey. Serves 10.

For streusel topping: In large bowl, stir together ¼ cup butter, ⅓ cup flour, ¼ cup sugar, ½ cup brown sugar, 1 teaspoon cinnamon, ¼ cup chopped pecans, and a pinch of nutmeg.

ISLAND HOUSE INN QUICK AND EASY CHEESECAKE

Vegetable oil
Graham cracker crumbs,
  ground very fine
2 pounds cream cheese, at
  room temperature

12 ½ ounces powdered
  sugar
5 eggs
2 teaspoons vanilla

Oil Bundt pan thoroughly and coat with crumbs, shaking excess crumbs out of pan. Set aside. In large mixer bowl, beat cream cheese until smooth; add sugar and beat until completely combined. In another bowl, whisk eggs with vanilla. Add to cream cheese mixture slowly, until completely combined. Pour into prepared pan, set pan in larger pan half filled with water, and bake at 350 degrees an hour, or until firm. Allow to stand for half an hour before serving.

THE PIONEER MILL INN
Tiffin

In the developing years of this country, mills were among the first signs of stability in a new settlement. There was a mill on nearly every little stream, with a huge water wheel powering grindstones that turned the farmer's wheat and corn into dietary staples.

Mills were meeting places, where isolated pioneers were glad to wait for their flour or meal, enjoying gossip and companionship. To avoid a long ride, many people settled near a mill, forming communities.

In 1822, Virginian Josiah Hedges laid out a town along the Sandusky River near his mill. His house was the first in the town he named for his friend, Edward Tiffin, first Governor of Ohio.

Mills were dry and dusty, and many were destroyed by fire. Hedges' mill burned in 1876, but was rebuilt as a three-story red brick structure, with turbines beneath the surface of the water powering the mill's grinding wheels.

A second fire burned the third floor in 1937, and it was not replaced, giving the building a truncated appearance. The Pioneer Milling Company continued in operation until the 1960s.

In 1974, it was converted to a restaurant by seven local men, who donated it to Tiffin University in 1985, to serve in the University's hotel/restaurant management program.

"It's been a very good program for us," said George Kidd, Tiffin University President. "The program will grow, and we can have an impact on the industry."

The Pioneer Mill, placed on the National Register in 1980, is nevertheless primarily a restaurant, and an attractive one. Its tall windows overlook a just-for-show mill wheel and the wooded island, with ducks squabbling in the millstream below. Partially plastered brick walls and fire-blackened beams in the bi-level dining room are decorated with mill equipment.

"A lot of places built twelve years ago need to be redecorated," said Michael Pinkston, manager of Pioneer Mill. "We don't have any of those problems here."

Pinkston wants the Pioneer Mill's food to be "real" and healthful. "Ninety per cent of everything we sell here is made here from raw ingredients," he said. He takes particular pride in the Sunday family-style dinner of "lumpy mashed potatoes," served with Swiss steak, baked ham, or roast chicken, with Grandma's Salad and peach crisp à la mode, for a very affordable price. "So a family can come, and children are accustomed to eating out," he explained.

Weekday luncheons offer hearty sandwiches on croissant or rye, specialty salads, or a generous buffet for plenty of choice. At dinner, Snapper Turtle soup and pasta appetizers lead an array of dinner salads, steaks, and imaginative entrées. Two favorites are salmon with julienne vegetables, baked in parchment paper, and Scallops William, with mushrooms and peppers, topped with Mozzarella. Daily specials might be grilled swordfish with lime Hollandaise, or red snapper Picasso, with nutmeg sauce and mandarin oranges.

A perfect Crème Brulée is the house dessert specialty, but you might want to sample Millstream Ice Cream Pie, a chocolate cookie shell filled with coffee and chocolate ice creams, Bailey's Irish Crème liqueur, and chocolate sauce.

The Pioneer Mill, 255 Riverside Drive, Tiffin, Ohio 44883, is open for lunch 11:30 a.m. to 2 p.m., Monday through Friday, for dinner 5:30 to 9 p.m., Monday through Friday, until 10 p.m. on Saturday, and for Sunday family-style dinner 12 Noon to 4 p.m., regular menu 4 to 8 p.m. (419)448-8662. Dress is casual, all legal beverages are served, including Sunday, and reservations are accepted, preferred for parties of 8 or more. A children's menu is available. AE, DC, MC, V. ($$$)

PIONEER MILL ONION SOUP

2 ½ pounds Spanish yellow
   onions, sliced
4 quarts beef stock
1 ⅓ Tablespoons Kitchen
   Bouquet

¾ cup Burgundy wine
Swiss cheese

Slice onions and place in large pot with stock. Bring to boil, add Kitchen Bouquet, remove from heat, and stir in wine. Cool, then refrigerate. Do not cover. To serve, bring to boil; top with Swiss cheese. Yields 16 8-ounce servings.

No Bland

6

PIONEER MILL CHICKEN MANDARIN SALAD

3 cups cooked, diced
   chicken breast
¾ cup pecan pieces
1 ½ cups mandarin
   oranges
1 ½ cup diced celery
1 ½ cup diced hard cooked
   eggs

3 cups mayonnaise
⅓ cup Thousand Island
   dressing
1 teaspoon curry powder
¾ teaspoon pepper

In large bowl, mix first 6 ingredients well. Blend remaining ingredients, add to chicken mixture, and stir just enough to moisten. Garnish with avocado or tomato. Serves 10 or 12.

PIONEER MILL CRÈME BRULÉE

4 cups heavy cream
¾ teaspoon vanilla
Pinch of salt
8 egg yolks

¾ cup + 2 Tablespoons
   brown sugar
Cinnamon

In heavy saucepan, combine cream with vanilla and salt. Heat slowly until surface shimmers, about 5 minutes. In large bowl, combine with egg yolks until blended; avoid air bubbles. Place 8 custard cups in roasting pan, and fill cups with custard. Pour warm water into pan halfway up cups, cover loosely with foil, and bake at 300 degrees an hour and 15 minutes, or until custard is firm around edges. Remove custards and refrigerate at least 3 hours. Before serving, top with brown sugar and a touch of cinnamon, and place under broiler to caramelize the sugar. Serves 8.

THE BOODY HOUSE RESTAURANT
Toledo

On the site where Major General "Mad" Anthony Wayne's Fort Industry defied the British in 1794, twelve contiguous commercial buildings were constructed between 1862 and 1897. Handsome four and five-story brick structures faced Summit Street; rear doors opened on the railroad at Water Street.

"This was Toledo," said Dr. Robert Hauman, who has helped to revitalize a deteriorated area that was once threatened by demolition.

The block was rescued and placed on the National Register in 1973, and renovation into unified office and retail space was begun in the late 1970s. Victorian facades were left intact, with an interior walkway and a four-story atrium connecting new offices. Materials from Toledo's lost historic buildings were incorporated as decorative and functional elements in new Fort Industry Square.

At the corner of Jefferson Street, an 1865 candy factory, later the Toledo Savings Bank, became The Boody House Restaurant, named for a famous Toledo hotel demolished in 1928.

"The bar was in the original Boody House," Dr. Hauman said, "and the chandeliers came from a bank. All the built-in bars are from Toledo buildings, and all the stained glass is from old houses in Toledo."

These artifacts create an atmosphere of elegance and history in a serious restaurant overlooking the Maumee River.

Contemporary American cuisine, under Chef John Mihaly, is varied and exciting. "You could come here every night in the week and have a different experience," he said. All foods are prepared to order, with sauces designed to enhance, not mask, the flavors of the freshest seafoods, meats, and produce, beautifully presented. "People eat with their eyes more than ever," Mihaly said.

Items on the menu— Duckling Hunter's Style, Chicken with Shrimp Courvoisier— are always present, but "Chef's Suggestions"— Paupiettes of Sole with sole mousse, boneless half chicken sautéed with calves liver— change constantly. Lunches are necessarily lighter, but begin with the same flavorful soups, and end with desserts ranging from fresh raspberries in English Cream to Dacquoise: layers of nut meringue sandwiched with meltingly rich chocolate buttercream.

The Boody House, 152 North Summit Street, Toledo, Ohio 43604, is open for lunch 11:30 a.m. to 3 p.m., Monday through Friday, for dinner 5:30 to 10 p.m. Monday through Friday, 6 to 10 p.m. Saturday. (419) 241-3322. Dress is "comfortable," all legal beverages are served, and there is an extensive wine list and 2 Cruvinet systems, providing many fine wines by the glass. Reservations are suggested, especially for dinner on weekends. AE, CB, DC, MC, V. ($$$)

BOODY HOUSE CORN CHOWDER

½ cup butter
½ cup flour (about)
2 cups yellow corn
1 quart clam juice
4 slices bacon
2 medium onions, diced
1 stalk celery, diced
¼ green pepper, diced
¼ red pepper, diced

2 medium potatoes, boiled
  and diced
1 quart cream
Juice of one lemon
Bay leaf
Thyme
White pepper
Flaked smoked fish as
  optional garnish

In small saucepan, melt butter and add flour slowly, whisking until mixture forms ball; all flour may not be needed. In another pan, boil corn in clam juice. In soup kettle, crisp bacon; pour off excess fat, add onion and celery, and sauté. Add peppers, then corn mixture, and boil, adding butter/flour mixture until desired consistency is achieved. Add potato and cream, season, and simmer 10 to 15 minutes. Serves 12.

BOODY HOUSE CHICKEN SALAD IN PINEAPPLE RING

3 pounds boneless,
  skinless chicken breast
1 bay leaf
1 Tablespoon black
  peppercorns
1 whole, fresh pineapple
½ cup diced celery
½ cup chopped pecans

2 cups mayonnaise (about)
Salt and pepper
Paprika
4 hard cooked eggs
12 tomato wedges
12 black olives
Leaf lettuce

In lightly salted water, poach chicken, bay leaf, and pepper-corns about 30 minutes. Cool and dice. Slice unpeeled pineapple ¾ inch thick, reserving leaves for garnish. Core slices, and remove rings of peel; set rings aside. Dice pineapple meat and set aside, reserving juice. In large bowl, combine chicken, celery, ½ cup pineapple, pecans, pineapple juice, and enough mayonnaise to moisten. Season. Present salad in pineapple ring on lettuce, garnished with tomatoes, eggs, olives, and pineapple chunks. Serves 4.

BOODY HOUSE HAZELNUT TORTE

14 ounces cake flour	20 ounces sugar
3 ounces cocoa powder	7 ounces shortening
¼ ounce baking soda	19 ounces milk
¼ ounce salt	5 eggs
½ ounce baking powder	1 capful vanilla

Sift dry ingredients into large mixer bowl. Add shortening in chunks, then slowly add 9 ounces milk and vanilla. Mix to batter consistency. Alternately add eggs and rest of milk, mixing well. Pour into greased, paper-lined, 10-inch cake pan. Bake at 325 degrees about 30 minutes, or until cake tester comes clean. Cut cake into 3 layers; spread 2 layers with filling (see below) and stack. Top with third layer, and glaze top and sides with frosting (see below). Garnish with hazelnuts dipped in white chocolate.

For filling: In large pan, bring 20 ounces heavy cream to boil; add 2 pounds white chocolate and melt. Pour mixture into bowl and stir until it begins to cool, then slowly add 6 ounces crushed, roasted hazelnuts.

For frosting: In saucepan, melt 12 ounces semi-sweet chocolate with 2 ounces butter over low heat.

ZENKO'S RIVER HOUSE
Perrysburg

During the war of 1812, Major General William Henry Harrison built a fort below the rapids of the Maumee, where he brought together fragments of several armies. Fort Meigs, named for Governor Return Johnathan Meigs, was repeatedly under siege by British and Indians during the winter and spring of 1813.

Just after the British were driven away from the fort, young Commodore Oliver Hazard Perry defeated a small British fleet on Lake Erie, and the British threat to Northern Ohio ended.

A town called "Orleans," near Fort Meigs, destroyed during the war, was rebuilt in 1820 and named for the hero of the naval battle. Perrysburg became an active port on Lake Erie, and substantial houses and business structures were erected in the prosperous little town.

Riverfront property in Perrysburg was bought by George Getz in the late 1860s, and on it he built a two-story red brick building that housed his home and a grocery store. A saloon, an oyster bar, and an ice cream parlor are also believed to have occupied the house while he owned it.

In 1897, the building was purchased by Dr. John Rheinfrank, whose brother, an architect, remodeled it into a hospital. The original L-shaped structure was considerably enlarged, and patients were treated for goiter, a thyroid disorder prevalent in the Great Lakes region, until 1955. As part of the Perrysburg Historic District, the building was placed on the National Register in 1975.

In 1986, John and Sue Hrosko, who operated a successful Perrysburg delicatessen, bought and remodeled the building. Small patient rooms were opened into large dining areas, and the upstairs converted into office suites, but the surgery, with its enormous skylight, was preserved, and now is a bright dining room filled with plants. Attractively decorated, with a pleasant, homelike atmosphere, Zenko's River House again welcomes those in search of food and spirits, and manager Mike Munz will take you on a guided tour.

Appetizers are particularly good and generous; escargot, oysters, prime rib kabobs, and a fruit and cheese sampler are unusual, and there are at least two homemade soups daily.

143

Salads, omelets, and quiches add to a vast array of sand-
wiches at lunchtime. Try the Maumee Muffin, with Provolone,
Cheddar, lettuce, tomato, and sprouts on a bun, or the "Best
Wurst in Town."

Dinner entrées include steaks, chops, pasta, chicken, ham—
baked in wine— seafood, and barbecue, plus more outstanding
sandwiches. There's no shortage of good desserts, either, with
different cheesecakes, Irish Whiskey Cake, strudel, and the
house specialty, Millionaire Pie. It's a luscious concoction of
cream, pineapple, peaches and lots of secret ingredients in a
crumb crust, and is as rich as its name implies.

Zenko's River House, 115 West Front Street, Perrysburg, Ohio 43551,
is open 11 a.m. to 10 p.m., Monday through Thursday, until 11 p.m. Friday
and Saturday, with continuous service. Dinner service begins at 5 p.m.,
and the Tavern remains open until 1 a.m. (419)874-1401. Dress is casual,
all legal beverages are served, and reservations are accepted. AE, MC, V.
($$)

ZENKO'S RIVER HOUSE MUSHROOMS AU VIN

3 Tablespoons melted
  butter, divided
2 cups whole, fresh
  mushroom caps

1 Tablespoon finely
  chopped parsley,
  divided
¼ cup dry white wine

In buttered sauté pan, place mushrooms, sprinkle with re-
maining butter and half the parsley, and sauté half a minute.
Add wine, flambé, and simmer until mushrooms are tender.
Serve hot with all juices, garnished with remaining parsley.
One serving.

ZENKO'S RIVER HOUSE GARDEN PASTA

24 ounces cooked
  fettuccine
⅔ cup sliced yellow squash
⅔ cup sliced zucchini
⅔ cup sliced onion
⅔ cup sliced mushrooms
⅔ cup sliced sweet red
  pepper

Butter for sautéeing
Marinara sauce (see
  below)
Grated Provolone cheese
Finely chopped parsley

In large skillet, sauté vegetables in butter until tender. To serve, divide fettuccine onto 4 ovenproof serving plates, ladle marinara sauce over noodles, top with a fourth of vegetables and grated cheese. Broil 1 minute, garnish with chopped parsley, and serve. Serves 4.

For marinara sauce: sauté 1 cup chopped onion, 6 minced garlic cloves, and ½ cup chopped parsley in 6 Tablespoons olive oil and 3 ounces butter for 5 minutes. Add 2 Tablespoons oregano flakes and salt and pepper to taste. Add 6 cups canned tomatoes, 2 cups tomato paste, and 2 cups water. Simmer about 30 minutes. Yields at least 10 to 12 servings.

ZENKO'S RIVER HOUSE VEAL PROVENÇALE

1 cup flour
Salt and pepper
Dash of thyme
2 pounds veal slices
1 cup sliced onion

2 cloves garlic, minced
3 Tablespoons chopped
  parsley
½ cup dry white wine
3 tomatoes, diced

Blend flour with seasonings, then dredge veal slices in seasoned flour. Melt butter in skillet and sauté veal quickly on both sides. Remove veal to warm platter. In pan drippings, sauté onion, garlic, and parsley for 1 to 2 minutes. Add wine and simmer until reduced by half. Add tomatoes and season with salt and pepper. Heat through, stirring often. To serve, divide veal slices onto 4 serving plates. Pour tomato mixture over veal and in circle around plate. Serve with side of fettuccine, and garnish with parsley. Serves 4.

THE CHADWICK INN
Maumee

Indian aggressiveness in the Northwest Territory spread during the early years of the United States; lack of game and an influx of settlers were an increasing irritation, and the frustrated Indians retaliated.

After a series of American defeats, President George Washington sent Major General "Mad" Anthony Wayne, a hero of the Revolution, into Ohio in the Spring of 1793. Working their way north from Cincinnati, Wayne and an army of 2,500 wintered at Fort Greene Ville, then built Fort Recovery on the banks of the Wabash, where St. Clair had been defeated two years earlier. They constructed Fort Defiance at the junction of the Auglaize and Maumee Rivers in July, 1794.

It was not only Indians who wanted to possess the important water route and the Maumee Valley; the British refortified an old French trading post they called Fort Miamis, just below the rapids of the Maumee on American land.

On August 20, 1794, when American forces and Indians incited by the British met in battle four miles away, the British stayed secure in their fort. The Battle of Fallen Timbers, named for trees felled by high winds, lasted less than an hour, and marked the end of Indian warfare in Ohio for sixteen years.

Two miles downstream from the battle site, the town of Maumee was laid out in 1817. A commercial building was erected in 1836 by Levi Beebe, adjacent to his successful hotel. The three-story Greek Revival structure had multiple entries for tenants— a lawyer, the post office, and stores— and its corner location was a landmark on the stagecoach route between Detroit and Fort Wayne.

The rest of the block was destroyed by a tornado in 1839, and the commercial building was used as a hotel until the 1920s. Later, a series of restaurants occupied the first floor.

The building was placed on the National Register in 1974, but when it was purchased by Jim and Sharon Hodulik in 1985, it had been empty for several years, damaged by fire and neglect. Jim and his brothers Joe and Steve, operators of Ole Buddies Catering Service, did a lot of restoration themselves, lowering floors in the basement, and repairing the burned second floor.

Named "The Chadwick Inn" for relatives, the decor reflects the 1830s, with teal, cream, and terra-cotta-colored papers and curtains. Antique cupboards display china, including the inn's custom-designed cover plates.

American Cuisine, with many dishes sanctioned by the American Heart Association, offers salads, sandwiches, and light entrées for lunch, while dinner emphasizes fresh seafood, veal, and the inn's famous prime rib. Lake Erie pickerel and perch are among entrées which may be sauteed, broiled, fried, or blackened to order; accompanying vegetables are crisp and delicious. An array of elegant desserts is presented on a tray for your selection— if you have room!

Chadwick Inn, 301 River Road, Maumee, Ohio 43537, is open for lunch 11 a.m. to 2 p.m., Monday through Friday, for dinner 5 to 10 p.m. Monday through Saturday, and 11 a.m. to 7 p.m. for the "Groaning Board" on Sundays, from Labor Day to Memorial Day; the inn is closed Sundays in summer. Luncheon menu and sandwiches are available in the bar during all open hours. (419)893-2388. Attire is casual to dressy. All legal beverages are served (only beer on Sunday), and reservations are accepted, but not required. MC, V, AE, and Discover. ($$$)

CHADWICK INN NEW ENGLAND CLAM CHOWDER

1 pint shucked clams OR 15-ounce can minced clams	½ cup chopped onion
	2 cups milk, divided
	1 cup light cream
4 ounces salt pork, diced	3 Tablespoons flour
4 cups diced potatoes	1 ½ teaspoons salt
1 ½ cups water	Dash of pepper

Dice clams and set aside, OR strain canned clams, reserving ½ cup liquid. In large pan, fry salt pork until crisp. Remove bits of pork and reserve. To pan drippings, add clam liquid, potatoes, water, and onion. Cook, covered, until potatoes are tender, about 20 minutes. Stir in clams, 1 ¾ cups milk, and cream. Blend remaining milk with flour, then stir into chowder. Cook and stir until boiling; season. Sprinkle salt pork bits on each serving. Serves 6.

CHADWICK INN STUFFED MUSHROOMS

24 silver dollar sized
  mushrooms
5 Tablespoons butter,
  divided
2 teaspoons green onions
  with tops, chopped
1 teaspoon lemon juice

1 cup king crab meat
½ cup soft breadcrumbs
1 egg, beaten
½ teaspoon dillweed
¼ cup dry white wine
¾ cup shredded jack
  cheese

Remove stems from mushrooms; chop stems, and place in pan with onions and 2 Tablespoons butter. Sauté until onions are soft. Remove from heat and add remaining ingredients, reserving ½ cup cheese. Mix well. Press mixture firmly into mushroom caps. Melt remaining butter in ovenproof pan. Place stuffed caps in pan; top with remaining cheese. These may be held for a day or two, refrigerated. Bake at 400 degrees about 15 minutes. Serves 6.

COLUMBIAN HOUSE
Waterville

Early exploration of Northwest Ohio was made difficult by the Great Black Swamp, which covered over two thousand square miles. Dense mosquitoes caused fever and sickness, and The Maumee River, with its many rapids, was the only way to travel through the swampy area. A huge limestone boulder on its shore was a landmark and meeting place for Indians and French explorers, who named it "Roche de Boeuf" (stone ox), possibly as early as the first quarter of the seventeenth century.

John Pray left Rhode Island in 1817 and settled in the lonely country near Roche de Boeuf, establishing the first grist mill in Northern Ohio on Granger Island in 1821. Travelers to the mill, and to his later ventures of a carding mill, a rope walk, and a distillery, needed a place to stay, and in 1828, Pray built the first portion of his inn. The Columbian House became an important stagecoach stop on the route between Dayton and Detroit, and a later, more impressive wing was completed about 1837. Now used as the front of the inn, this section was built chiefly of black walnut, and incorporated elements of both Federal and Greek Revival styles.

Among the original twenty-three rooms were a taproom, a post office, a general store, kitchens, dining rooms, and a ladies' parlor, with bedrooms and a small jail on the second floor, and an enormous ballroom on the third floor.

After Pray's death in 1872, the tavern lost its importance in the community, and the building was used as a dressmaker's shop, a milliner's shop, and a school, before standing empty for several years around the turn of the century. It was restored in the 1920s and used as an antiques shop until the late 1930s; at that time it was again empty and had fallen into disrepair when purchased by Ethel Nelson Arnold in 1943.

Wartime restrictions on building materials and a shortage of labor caused a three-year delay before Mrs. Arnold was able to open the lower two floors as a warm-weather restaurant. The third floor ballroom was later restored, and the building was placed on the National Register in 1969.

Catering to area clubs and those who appreciated her collection of antiques, Mrs. Arnold offered "Home-cooked meals" that gained a wide reputation for The Columbian House. Its popularity grew, and after her death, her son George and his wife Jacqueline took over its management, installing central heating in 1971 in order to stay open through the winter.

The wonderful old building retains its coziness, with seating in four antique-filled rooms. "We try to avoid the appearance of being a commercial restaurant," Jacqueline Arnold said, and the tearoom-style luncheon menu adds to the homey atmosphere. An assortment of salads is joined by sandwiches and entrées of Chicken à la King and Shrimp Newburg, with homemade corn sticks.

Dinner entrées are more elaborate, including a Vegetarian Plate, Ham in Orange Sauce, Roast Chicken and Dressing (there's Ham AND Chicken, if you can't decide) Shrimp Curry over Rice, choices of fish and crab, and prime rib and steaks. All entrées are served with vegetables, the inn's famous Tomato Pudding, salad, potato, and hot bread and butter. Always available are delicate Soup Romaine and a selection of old-fashioned desserts such as meringues filled with ice cream and strawberries, brownies à la mode with homemade chocolate sauce, and Double Chocolate Mousse— Chocolate, chocolate chip mousse served in a chocolate shell, topped with whipped cream.

Columbian House, 3 North River Road, Waterville, Ohio 43566, is open for lunch Tuesday through Saturday, 11:30 a.m. to 2 p.m., for dinner Tuesday through Friday 6 to 9 p.m., and on Saturday 5:30 to 9:30. (419)878-3006. Dress is casual, all legal beverages are served, and reservations are encouraged, especially Saturday nights and during the month of December. Columbian House is closed most of the month of January. AE, CB, MC, V. ($$)

COLUMBIAN HOUSE CANDIED ORANGES

6 oranges   **4 cups water**
4 cups sugar

In saucepan, simmer whole oranges until their skin is slightly soft; this removes bitterness. Cool under cold water.

In another large saucepan, bring sugar and water to a boil. Cut oranges into 12 wedges each and add to syrup. Turn heat as low as possible and simmer 2 or 3 hours, until skins are almost transparent.

Use oranges as garnish; syrup may be used to flavor ham or to glaze duck.

COLUMBIAN HOUSE MERINGUE SHELLS

3 egg whites
¼ teaspoon cream of
tartar

1 cup sugar

In large bowl, beat egg whites and cream of tartar until frothy; gradually beat in sugar a little at a time. Beat until very stiff and glossy. Drop ⅓ cup meringue on heavy brown paper on baking sheet. With the back of a spoon, make a depression in the center.

Bake 60 minutes at 275 degrees; turn off oven and leave meringues in oven until cool. Serve, filled with ice cream and topped with fruit, or chocolate or butterscotch sauce.

LA ROE'S GRAND RAPIDS
Grand Rapids

About twenty-five miles southwest of Toledo, the Maumee River widens, rushing over Wolf Rapids and surrounding two small islands. In 1833, New Englander John N. Graham purchased land here to plat a village; he also built a dam and a mill that produced both lumber and cornmeal.

The village of Gilead, near the site of several earlier Indian encampments, grew rapidly after the Providence Dam was built in 1845, becoming a port on the Miami, Wabash, and Erie Canal. The original millrace and dam were destroyed, but the "Gilead Side-Cut" of the canal created the most powerful water power in the country. A larger mill was built in 1848, to take advantage of the water power, and it attracted a great deal of business and new residents to the area.

By 1868, the town had outgrown its name, and became "Grand Rapids.'

W.E. Kerr was twenty years old when he came to Grand Rapids to work for his brother, the town's leading merchant. As bookkeeper, then traveling salesman, he accumulated funds to open a small general store, which he built on Front Street in the late 1880s. In 1894, he doubled the size of the building, creating an attractive Italianate commercial building of dark red brick, with a decorative brickwork cornice.

The building housed the Oddfellows' hall on its second floor, and was later a grocery, but it fell on hard times and had become a rough tavern when David La Roe bought it in 1974. He took off aluminum siding, tore out cheap paneling, and created a banquet room/theatre from the old lodge hall.

La Roe's is one of many restored buildings in a charming Victorian village, where you may walk on the old canal towpath, look at interesting commercial and residential architecture, ride on an excursion passenger train, and visit many unusual shops. "Step back and relax a little bit," David La Roe said.

His restaurant is a great place to do just that, and to enjoy a good meal in a pleasant gallery atmosphere. Works by local artists grace exposed brick walls in the dining room, enhanced by floods of light from huge front windows.

And the food is no less agreeable, especially if you like

juicy, meaty, barbecued country ribs, served every night. This is not just a rib house, however; there's baked chicken, ham Hawaiian, shrimp, steaks, and a salad bar, plus great homemade soups— the cream of corn is particularly good— and nice hot breads. La Roe's serves breakfast, and lunch features sandwiches, salads, and burgers, with "munchies" for starters or in between, and a dinner buffet on weekends. Desserts are terrific anytime, including a dynamite peanut butter streusel pie.

La Roe's Restaurant, Front Street, Grand Rapids, Ohio 43522, is open 7 days a week, 8 a.m. to 10 p.m., with continuous service. (419)832-3082. Dress is casual, all legal beverages are served, including Sunday, reservations are accepted, and a children's menu is available. Dinner buffet is open Friday and Saturday nights, in addition to regular menu, and Girty's Back Stage Dinner Theatre is open during the month of December each year. No credit cards are accepted. ($$)

LA ROE'S VEGETABLE DIP

⅔ cup Miracle Whip
⅔ cup sour cream
1 Tablespoon dried onion
1 Tablespoon Lawry's
  seasoning salt
1 Tablespoon parsley

1 Tablespoon dill weed
1 Tablespoon MSG
1 Tablespoon + 1 ½
  teaspoons
  Worcestershire sauce
2 dashes Tabasco

In bowl, thoroughly mix all ingredients. Flavor is better if allowed to stand overnight in refrigerator. Serve with sliced or julienne vegetables as dip.

LA ROE'S PINEAPPLE SAUCE

One 8 ½-ounce can
  crushed pineapple
1 cup brown sugar
2 Tablespoons lemon juice

1 Tablespoon yellow
  mustard
¼ teaspoon salt

In saucepan, mix all ingredients, heat to simmer, and add enough cornstarch (mixed with some of the pineapple juice) to thicken. Serve with baked or fried ham.

156

LA ROE'S STRAWBERRY PIE

One 9-inch baked pie shell
1 ½ quarts strawberries
½ cup water
1 cup sugar

3 Tablespoons cornstarch
1 Tablespoon butter
Whipped cream for
  garnish

Wash and cap berries, and place 1 cup berries, crushed, in saucepan with water sugar, and cornstarch. Cook over medium heat until transparent, add butter, and cool. Place whole berries in pie shell, and pour cooked berries over them. Refrigerate to set, and serve topped with whipped cream. Serves 8.

THE GOLDEN LAMB
Lebanon

Ohio became a state in February, 1803. Warren County was formed in May, and in December, Jonas Seaman obtained a license to operate his two-story log tavern in newly laid-out Lebanon, Warren's county seat. Located at the corner of Main and Broadway, Seaman's tavern was a popular meeting place for local businessmen and passing travelers.

"A new and commodious brick building" replaced the log tavern about 1815, the north wing was built in 1854, and a fourth story was added about 1878. Business was conducted by a succession of owners as "Henry Share's Tavern," "Bradley House," "Stubbs House," and "Lebanon House," and although the name "The Golden Lamb" first appeared in a newspaper advertisement in 1826, it was probably in use long before that time— few of Ohio's early residents could read, and colorful signs were easily recognized.

Henry Clay, Daniel Webster, and William Henry Harrison were frequent visitors to The Golden Lamb, and Charles Dickens stopped during his 1842 tour of the United States. Statesmen, authors, educators and ten U.S. presidents have been guests, and nineteen overnight rooms named and decorated in their honor are presently open to public view when not occupied.

In 1926, new owner Robert H. Jones renovated The Golden Lamb and furnished it with antiques, including his fine collection of Shaker furniture. He operated the business until 1969, when it came under the management of Cincinnati's famed Comisar family. Certified as Ohio's oldest continuous business, The Golden Lamb was placed on the National Register in 1978.

Always noted for its bountiful table, The Golden Lamb continues in that tradition under Chef Erwin Pfeil, who changes the menu every day, and braises, roasts, and poaches fresh meats and seafoods in season, as was done a hundred years ago.

Luncheon might be braised beef tips in red wine sauce with fresh mushrooms, a savory lamb stew with dumplings, an omelet or one of two fish dishes. Dinner entrées of duck, turkey, and pork loin are always offered, and include relish, appetizer,

159

salad, two vegetables, and beverage; "Lighter Fare" and Sunday "Petite Dinners" eliminate some extras at a reduced cost, but nobody ever leaves hungry— not with fresh hot bread and spicy apple butter on the tables!

Dessert menus, changed quarterly, reflect seasonal availability. Recurring favorites are Boston Cream Pie oozing rich filling and iced with chocolate; fresh fruit cobblers; and Sister Lizzie's Shaker Sugar Pie, a simple concoction of brown sugar, cream, and butter that melts on the tongue.

The Golden Lamb, 27 S. Broadway, Lebanon, Ohio 45036, is open for breakfast on Sunday only, 8 to 10 a.m.; for lunch 11 a.m. to 3 p.m. Monday through Saturday; and for dinner 5 to 9 p.m. Monday through Thursday, until 10 p.m. Friday and Saturday. Sunday dinner is served from 12 Noon until 8 p.m., Sunday brunch (not buffet) from 12 Noon until 3 p.m. The Black Horse Tavern is open 11 a.m. to 11:30 p.m. Monday through Thursday, to 12:30 a.m. Friday and Saturday, and from 1 to 9 p.m. on Sunday. 19 rooms available for overnight guests. (513)932-5065. Dress code prohibits "muscle" shirts, "cut-off" shorts, and bare feet, as well as shorts after 6 p.m. on weekends. All legal beverages are served, including Sunday, and there is an extensive wine list. Reservations are necessary for all meals except breakfast, and for overnight. AE, CB, DC, MC, V. ($$$)

GOLDEN LAMB PEANUT SOUP

1 medium onion, chopped	**2 cups smooth peanut**
2 ribs celery, chopped	**butter**
¼ cup butter	**1 ¾ cups light cream**
3 Tablespoons flour	**Chopped peanuts**
2 quarts chicken stock	

Sauté onion and celery in butter until soft, but not brown. Blend in flour, add chicken stock, stirring constantly, and bring to a boil. Pour through a sieve, add peanut butter and cream, stirring to blend. Return to low heat, but do not boil. Serve, garnished with chopped peanuts. This soup is also good served cold. Serves 10.

GOLDEN LAMB HANCOCK SHAKER CHICKEN SPINACH PUDDING

4 cups diced, cooked chicken
3 cups chopped, cooked spinach, flavored with rosemary
1 cup cubed Cheddar cheese
3 Tablespoons butter
1 teaspoon salt
1 teaspoon pepper
1 teaspoon dry mustard
1 teaspoon scraped raw onion
3 Tablespoons flour
2 cups milk
Day-old bread for "lid'
Butter

In a greased 3-quart baking dish, mix chicken, spinach, and ½ cup cheese. In a saucepan, melt butter and stir in seasonings and flour, then milk. Cook four or five minutes, stirring constantly. Add remaining cheese and pour over chicken mixture. Arrange pieces of bread to cover top of mixture about 1-inch thick, and butter well. Bake at 350 degrees for 20 minutes, or until heated through and brown on top. Serves 8.

GOLDEN LAMB OSGOOD PIE

One 9-inch unbaked pie shell
½ cup raisins, cooked until plump
½ cup peeled, cored, chopped apples
½ cup chopped nuts
½ cup melted margarine
2 eggs, beaten
1 ½ teaspoons vinegar
1 cup sugar

Mix all ingredients in a large bowl. Pour into pie shell and bake at 375 degrees for 40 minutes. Cool well before serving. Serves 8.

PEERLESS MILL INN
Miamisburg

$\mathbf{L}$ong before white men came to the beautiful Miami River valley, prehistoric Adena Indians chose it as the site of their great Miamisburg Mound. Miami Indians, driven west by more warlike tribes, were followed by scattered pioneers who never owned the land they worked.

Many of the first permanent settlers were Germans from Pennsylvania, who floated down the Ohio River, then trekked overland. Four of these founded Miamisburg in 1818, platting a town of ninety lots on the bank of the Miami.

When the Miami and Erie Canal was opened in 1828, it brought commerce and prosperity, and by mid-century, Miamisburg was a thriving manufacturing center.

On the east bank of Lock 26 in Miamisburg, a flour mill and a sawmill were built in the 1820s, powered by canal waters. Under a succession of owners, the flour mill continued in operation until 1938.

The sawmill had ceased operation and was used for grain storage when Peerless Waters, son-in-law of owner Uriah Engleman, converted it to a restaurant called "Peerless Pantry," in 1929. Under four owners, it has been skillfully enlarged, retaining its cozy charm, although the flour mill is gone, and the canal is now a parking lot.

Don and Barbara Walsh bought The Peerless Mill Inn in 1980, and, with the culinary expertise of Chef Jim Keadey, have made it one of the most popular restaurants in the Miami Valley. A low, rambling structure, with worn stone floors in the oldest portion, its unexpected nooks house antiques and artifacts, and the feeling of warmth and intimacy is enhanced by seasonal wood fires in four massive fireplaces.

"We take a great deal of pride in maintaining its heritage,' Barbara said. "We feel it is an important thing we are entrusted with."

And the food is of paramount concern. "A concerted effort is made," Don said, "to provide fresh meats, vegetables, our own baking, fresh seafoods from Boston, and dairy products. Nothing beats heavy whipping cream— we go through a hundred quarts a week." A lot of it ends up in the inn's outstanding soups and chowders; don't miss them!

Luncheon might be a salad of crabmeat and artichokes,

one of the dishes sanctioned by the American Heart Association, or a Ruffino Sandwich of Italian sausage, spinach, marinara sauce, and cheeses. Numerous dinner choices include
Roast Duckling and Veal Gruyere; all come with seven-layer
salad and vegetable, and some of the best hot rolls ever. Desserts include luscious pies and cobblers, cheesecakes, and the
favorite: an ice cream ball rolled in pecans and topped with
gooey hot fudge.

Peerless Mill Inn, 319 South Second Street, Miamisburg, Ohio 45342,
is open for lunch 11 a.m. to 2 p.m., Tuesday through Friday, for dinner 5
to 9 p.m., Tuesday through Thursday, 5 to 10 p.m. Friday and Saturday,
and 1 to 7 p.m. on Sunday, when there is a brunch buffet from 11 a.m. to
2 p.m. (513)866-5968. Dress is casual, all legal beverages are served, including Sunday, and there is a carefully selected wine list. Reservations are
suggested, especially weekends, and required on holidays. Children's prices
are available. AE, DC, MC, V, Discover. ($$$)

PEERLESS MILL INN BROCCOLI AND MUSHROOM CHOWDER

¾ cup butter
1 cup chopped celery
½ cup chopped onion
¾ cup flour
1 quart milk
1 quart half-and-half
  cream
1 bunch broccoli, chopped

2 cups chicken stock
2 cups cooked, cubed
  potatoes
1 pound mushrooms,
  quartered
1 teaspoon tarragon
Salt and pepper

In heavy 6-quart pan, melt butter; sauté celery and onions
until tender. Remove from heat, stir in flour, cook 1 or 2
minutes, and stir in milk and half-and-half. In smaller pot,
cook broccoli in stock, then add 1 cup broccoli stock to larger
pot. Add vegetables and seasonings to soup, simmer 10 min-
utes and serve. Garnish with parsley, broccoli floret, or fresh
tarragon.

PEERLESS MILL INN COTTAGE DILL ROLLS

2 ½ ounces yeast
6 ounces warm water
3 cups cottage cheese
2 ½ ounces sugar
2 ½ ounces onion,
   processed to liquid
1 ½ ounces butter
1 teaspoon salt

1 teaspoon baking soda
3 large eggs
1 ounce horseradish
½ ounce fresh dill
2 pounds flour
Melted butter
Kosher salt

Dissolve yeast in water. Mix together next eight ingredients, add yeast mixture, dill, and flour to make a soft dough. Knead until smooth. Cover and let dough rise 30 to 45 minutes. Form into rolls and allow to rise again. Bake at 400 degrees until golden. Brush with melted butter and sprinkle with Kosher salt. Yields 6 dozen.

PEERLESS MILL INN APPLE DUMPLING CAKE

1 ½ cups oil
3 eggs
2 cups sugar
2 teaspoons vanilla
3 cups flour
1 teaspoon baking soda

1 teaspoon salt
1 teaspoon cinnamon
3 cups diced apples, not
   peeled
1 cup nuts

In large bowl, mix oil, eggs, sugar, and vanilla. Add dry ingredients and mix well, then add apples and nuts. Pour into greased Bundt pan or 9" x 13" pan and bake at 350 degrees for 1 hour. Pour icing over hot cake at once.

For icing: Mix together 1 cup brown sugar, ¼ cup milk, and ½ cup melted butter.

THE FLORENTINE HOTEL
Germantown

In the valley formed by Little Twin Creek and Big Twin Creek, the first real settlers were Germans from Berks County, Pennsylvania, who had maintained their culture and religion, and spoke the German language. In the spring of 1804, Philip Gunckel, a miller, led a group down the Ohio River to Cincinnati, and then into the Miami Valley.

With typical German industry, they cooperated in clearing the lands they had bought, raising cabins and planting crops. By 1806, there were more than three hundred German-speaking people in the valley.

Gunckel, an important landowner and force in the community, operated a general store and grist mill, and was Justice of the Peace. In 1814, he platted thirty-two acres into a town, and on a lot on Market street, about 1816, he built a two-story brick tavern, leaving the bark on the huge joists, and installing a German-style beer cellar.

The property changed hands and names many times, with the present entrance wing constructed some time before 1850, and the name, "The Florentine Hotel," acquired around the turn of the century.

A popular social center for the town as well as for transients, the hotel began to deteriorate with prohibition, and was closed in 1974. As part of the Germantown Historic District, it was placed on the National Register in 1976, and was purchased for restoration that same year.

Today, it has an informal charm in the rustic tavern, where massive beams support a ceiling that has been opened to make room for an enormous back bar. At the rear of the room is the fireplace of the original tavern. Across the hall, with its handsome staircase, three rooms have been opened into one, where brick "nogging" is visible between structural members.

The Florentine Hotel re-opened as a restaurant in 1979, and was purchased by the Zimmerman family in 1985. Very much a family business, it is operated by Chef John, manager Trey, and Karl, who has recently joined to develop retail aspects.

"A lot of our cooking here reflects our own personal tastes,"

Chef John said. "We're tending toward leaner and lighter meals."

Fresh fish entrées reflect this trend; The Florentine has more than a half-dozen seafood entrées every night, plus poultry, steaks, pork chops, and, on weekends, the special roasted prime rib. For those with smaller appetites, petite portions are offered, and "Early Diners" may enjoy a smaller meal at a reduced price.

A nice selection of appetizers, soups, and salads round out a good meal, and the twice-baked potatoes and sautéed vegetables are especially good.

The two house-specialty desserts are noteworthy: Strawberries Rebecca is topped with a sour cream, rum-raisin sauce, and the rich Chocolate Mousse contains Kahlúa and Bailey's Irish Crème liqueur. They're not intoxicating, but are definitely habit-forming.

The Florentine Hotel, 21 West Market Street, Germantown, Ohio 45327, is open for lunch 11:30 a.m. to 2 p.m., Tuesday through Friday, and for dinner 4:30 to 9 p.m. Tuesday through Thursday, Friday and Saturday until 10 p.m. Sunday Brunch is 10 a.m. to 2 p.m., and dinner is 12 Noon to 7:15 p.m. Early Diners' Specials, at a reduced price, are served 4:30 to 6 p.m. (513)855-7225. Dress is casual to formal, all legal beverages are served, including Sunday, and reservations are suggested, requested for parties of 6 or more. Children's menu is available. MC, V. ($$$)

FLORENTINE HOTEL TOMATO AND SQUASH VINAIGRETTE

4 large tomatoes, diced
4 large yellow squash OR zucchini OR combination of the two, diced
1 teaspoon chopped basil
1 teaspoon chopped parsley
¼ cup minced onion
1 ½ teaspoons granulated garlic
4 ounces Wishbone Italian Dressing
¼ cup water
1 ounce reconstituted lemon juice
Salt and fresh ground pepper

In large bowl, fold together tomatoes and squash. Sprinkle with basil, parsley, onion, and garlic. In blender, emulsify

168

dressing, water, and lemon juice; pour over vegetables, add salt sparingly and lots of fresh ground pepper. Serves at least 12.

FLORENTINE HOTEL SEAFOOD CHOWDER

½ cup diced carrot
½ cup diced onion
½ cup diced celery
½ cup diced flounder (two 4-ounce filets)
1 cup diced pollock (two 8-ounce filets)
1 cup canned clam stock
1 cup milk
6 ounces butter
6 ounces flour
Salt and pepper
1 Tablespoon chopped parsley
1 teaspoon garlic powder

In soup pot over medium-high heat, place vegetables, fish, clam stock and milk. In skillet, melt butter, add flour, and cook roux several minutes, until it bubbles and has a nutty aroma. Add to steaming liquid and bring to boil, stirring constantly. Reduce heat, add seasonings, parsley, and garlic. Serve or refrigerate. To reheat, thin with equal parts water and milk; adjust seasoning. Serves 4.

FLORENTINE HOTEL SCALLOPED PINEAPPLE

4 heaping cups torn fresh bread, including crusts
14 to 16-ounce can crushed pineapple
4 eggs
¼ cup sugar
Pinch of salt
1 ½ cups milk
¼ cup melted butter

In large bowl, stir together bread and pineapple. In another bowl, beat eggs with sugar and salt, then add milk. Combine mixtures and add butter. Pour into greased 2-quart casserole and bake 30 to 35 minutes at 325 to 350 degrees. Serve as a side dish with meats, especially ham. Serves 16 to 20.

SHIELD'S CROSSING
Loveland

The scenic Little Miami River Valley first attracted settlers in 1796. It was an area of well-to-do farms until mid-nineteenth century railroad development made Loveland a "bedroom town" for wealthy Cincinnati businessmen.

One of these, Edward M. Shield, had owned foundries in Cincinnati. He retired in 1851, and represented various area foundries in Washington, D.C., where he obtained contracts for military equipment to be used during the Civil War. In 1873, he began the Mount Adams and Eden Park Inclined Railway Company.

In 1868, Mr. Shield purchased a two-story, L-shaped frame house in Loveland, on four acres overlooking the Little Miami. He named the estate "Christeen," and here he entertained lavishly until his death in 1879.

The property passed out of the Shield family in 1887, and although it was altered in the 1920s, the house and its six outbuildings had changed little when it became a restaurant in 1979. It was placed on the National Register in 1982.

Shield's Crossing welcomes guests with four spacious dining rooms opening off a wide hall. Upstairs, former bedrooms house the Christeen Gallery, with works of local artists on display.

Owner Mary Louise Davis likes to carry on Mr. Shield's tradition of hospitality. "Food is such an adventure," she said. "It's meant to be enjoyed with your friends and family. That's what we try to do here."

With Chef Gary Chalfin, she succeeds admirably. All foods are cooked to order, and unusual touches add to the homelike feeling. Sliced anise bread and homemade wine jelly are served before you order, diets are catered to, and "Twilight Meals," feature a special meal at a reduced price.

Luncheon soups, salads, and sandwiches are light and different— Gazebo Chicken Salad with walnuts, celery, and pineapple, a Reuben on a croissant, plus a different fresh seafood every day. Luncheon is served on the verandah in season.

Dinner might begin with oysters poached in white wine and garlic butter, or Fresh Vegetable Tempura. Seafood Chowder, available on weekends, is chunky with tomato and vegetables surrounding baby oysters and seafood. Entrées include steaks, trout stuffed with shrimp and spinach and baked in puff pastry, Veal Scaloppine, and Sweetbreads à la Maison, the house specialty, sautéed and served on fresh spinach.

Desserts vary, but frequent appearances are made by cheesecake with apricot sauce and almonds, a banana split in an eclair, and a light, delicate, peanut butter chiffon pie mounded with whipped cream.

Shield's Crossing, 220 Riverside Drive, Loveland, Ohio 45140, may be reached from exit #52 off I-275, or the Fields-Ertel exit off I-71. It is open for lunch 11:30 a.m. to 2:30 p.m., Tuesday through Friday, for dinner 5:30 to 10 p.m. Tuesday through Friday, until 11 p.m. on Saturday. Sunday Brunch is 10:30 a.m. to 2:30 p.m., except during the winter months, and Sunday dinner is 4:30 to 8 p.m. It is closed the week of July 4. (513)683-8220. "Dressy casual" attire is suggested, all legal beverages are served, including Sunday, and reservations are accepted. AE, CB, DC, MC, V. ($$$)

SHIELD'S CROSSING ANGEL HAIR PASTA WITH FRESH SALMON

½ medium red onion, diced
2 Tablespoons butter
½ pound mushrooms, sliced
1 Tablespoon flour
⅓ cup white wine
2 cups heavy cream, heated
Pinch fresh lemon thyme (or dried thyme or basil or sorrel)

½ pound fresh salmon, in julienne
1 medium tomato, diced
Salt and white pepper
1 pound fresh angel hair pasta
2 scallions, chopped

In deep pan, boil lightly salted water for pasta. In medium pan, sauté onion in butter until golden; add mushrooms and cook 1 minute, then add flour and stir to make a roux. Add wine and cream, stirring constantly. Add herbs, salmon, tomato, and seasonings and simmer 5 minutes. Slowly add pasta to boiling water, stirring occasionally. Cook about 4 minutes and drain. Ladle sauce over pasta and sprinkle with scallions. Serves 6 as appetizer, 4 as entree.

SHIELD'S CROSSING CHICKEN FRAMBOISE

8 skinless, boneless breasts of chicken
Flour for dredging
Salt and white pepper
Butter for sautéeing

⅓ cup raspberry vinegar
3 cups heavy cream ½ cup raspberry liqueur
2 cups fresh raspberries

Pound chicken lightly between wax paper, season and dredge in flour, shaking off excess. In skillet, sauté chicken in butter over medium heat until just brown. Remove chicken and discard butter. Deglaze pan with vinegar and reduce until syrupy. Add cream and liqueur, return chicken to pan, and simmer until sauce thickens. Adjust seasoning. Add raspberries and heat through. Remove chicken, arrange over wild rice, and spoon sauce over, being careful not to break up berries. Serves 8.

SHIELD'S CROSSING LEMON SOUFFLE

1 stick butter
1 ½ cups sugar
Juice of 4 lemons
Zest of 2 lemons

6 eggs, beaten
2 cups heavy cream, whipped

In double boiler over simmering water, melt butter. In bowl, mix sugar, lemon juice and zest. Add mixture and eggs to butter and whisk about 5 minutes or until thickened. Remove from heat and set over ice to cool. Fold whipped cream into cooled lemon mixture. Spoon or pipe into goblets and garnish with lemon twists and fresh mint. Serves 8 to 10.

THE MILLCROFT
Milford

Many Cincinnati area settlers came down the Ohio from Pennsylvania; Christian Waldschmidt, a veteran of the Revolution, led an advance party of about a dozen men from Reading and Lancaster to the Little Miami River in 1794. Waldschmidt purchased some 1100 acres, and returned with his family in 1796, to establish a community and a mill at New Germany, now Camp Dennison.

His daughter Catherine married one of his employees, Matthias Kugler, and they inherited Waldschmidt's sizeable empire of mills, warehouses, and land in 1814. Under Kugler's management, the holdings increased, with grist, saw, paper, and oil mills, all powered by the Little Miami, and a distillery. In 1827, Kugler purchased an imposing 1816 house across the river to the south— for use as a store.

The two-story Federal style frame structure was completed and enlarged, and was later the residence of the Kugler's son John and his wife Rebecca, until her death in 1872.

The Millcroft has been a restaurant since 1939, but has had several periods of neglect. After restoration, it received the 1979 Miami Purchase Historic Preservation Award.

Stephen and Pam Gongola brought years of restaurant experience when they took over operation of The Millcroft in 1985. The lovely old house once again has a homey atmosphere, with comfortable wing chairs and love seats in the dark green lounge. Several dining rooms and a shady terrace provide a choice of seatings for a memorable meal.

"We care about our customers," Pam said. "I feel I've invited someone to lunch or dinner in my home."

The Millcroft's American Cuisine entrées of veal, beef, pork, poultry, and seafood, include salad, a kettle of homemade soup (tomato clam broth is unusually good), rolls, and vegetable, and there are always exciting special or seasonal dishes as well. Highly recommended are Trout with Pecan Butter and Artichoke Hearts, and Sesame Chicken with Cumberland Sauce. At lunch, choose from light entrées, salads and sandwiches— you can even "build your own" sandwich from a list of favorites— and top it off with a brownie sundae, apple pie with ice cream, or Mocha Swirl Cheesecake.

The Tavern, in former stables, has an informal atmosphere

and features a limited menu of appetizers and hearty sandwiches, and a jazz trio to dance to on weekend nights.

The Millcroft, 203 Mill Street, Milford, Ohio 45150, is open 7 days a week. Lunch is 11 a.m. to 3 p.m., dinner 5 to 10 p.m. Monday through Thursday, to 11 p.m. Friday and Saturday, and Sunday Brunch is 11 a.m. to 3 p.m. The Tavern is open 11 a.m. to 1:30 a.m., with continuous service. (513)831-8654. Most men wear jackets and ties in the restaurant; tavern dress is casual. All legal beverages are served, including Sunday, and there is an extensive wine list. Reservations are recommended. AE, DC, MC, V. ($$$)

MILLCROFT SILVER SALMON WITH ARTICHOKE HEARTS

Two 7-ounce skinless, boneless silver salmon
4 ounces white wine
8 Tablespoons unsalted butter
3 medium mushrooms, sliced thin
4 artichoke hearts, halved lengthwise
Salt and pepper

Grill salmon over medium flame; do not overcook. In saute pan, reduce wine by one third. Stir in butter, add mushrooms and artichoke hearts, and sauté until warm. Season. Place salmon on serving plate and spoon sauce over. Serves 2.

MILLCROFT PORK SCALLOPINE WITH COARSE MUSTARD SAUCE

1 ¼ to 1 ½ pound pork tenderloin
2 ounces olive oil
Flour for dusting
Splash of white wine
½ cup heavy cream
1 Tablespoon Pommery mustard
Pinch of parsley
Rosemary or chives for garnish

Trim tenderloin thoroughly, and cut into one-inch pieces, about 2 ounces each. Carefully pound flat, and dust with flour. In skillet, heat olive oil hot, add pork, and cook 1 minute per side, or until lightly browned. Drain excess oil, deglaze skillet with wine and reduce by one fourth, then add cream and mustard and reduce until thick. Add parsley and serve with pork. Garnish with herbs. Serves 4.

MILLCROFT LOUISIANA GUMBO

½ frying chicken, cut up
Cayenne pepper and granulated garlic, for dusting
½ cup flour
¼ teaspoon granulated garlic
¼ teaspoon thyme
¼ teaspoon oregano
¼ teaspoon basil
½ teaspoon cayenne pepper

1 cup vegetable oil
1 medium Spanish onion, chopped
1 bell pepper, chopped
4 okra pods, sliced
1 rib celery
2 cups hot chicken stock
¼ pound Andouille or Kielbasa sausage, chopped

Dust chicken with pepper and garlic. Mix flour with herbs, flour chicken, and brown on both sides in hot oil, 20 to 25 minutes. Remove chicken from bones, and chop coarsely. Add remaining flour to oil in pan and stir over low heat until a black roux is formed. Do not burn! Add vegetables and cook about 5 minutes, stirring, then add chicken stock a little at a time, stirring. Add sausage and chicken and simmer about 20 minutes. Adjust seasoning. Serve with cooked rice or black beans and cornbread. Serves 6 or 8.

THE HERITAGE
Cincinnati

In 1827, Edgar and Martha Scott built a two-story, L-shaped brick house twelve miles east of Cincinnati. Constructed in the Federal style of bricks burned on the site, the house remained the Scott home until 1850.

The Cincinnati, Columbus, and Wooster Turnpike passed in front of the house; later, the Little Miami Railroad did also, and the neighborhood changed. Around the turn of the century, the house became a roadhouse, operated by Frank "Pretty" Kelley and his wife, "Ma" Kelley. Known as "Kelley's Gardens," it attracted sports figures, politicians, circus people, and nearly everyone else in the Cincinnati area looking for a wild time.

When Pretty died (perhaps not of natural causes) in 1919, Ma and their son, "Corny" continued, despite Prohibition, to operate the roadhouse.

According to legend, Corny served the wrong man one night, and Kelley's Gardens closed forever. The house, flooded to the second story during the 1937 flood, was repaired to become a perfectly respectable restaurant called "The Cottage," for twenty years.

In 1959, it was bought and renamed "The Heritage" by Jan and Howard Melvin. They have returned the house to its early elegance, while evolving a menu that ranges from simple, American cooking to the latest in innovative food.

Their search for local meats and produce led to a flexible menu that required a blackboard; in their travels, they discovered new foods and preparation methods to try. A shortage of fresh herbs prompted Jan to start a herb garden, and when Chef Jerry Hart joined them, he and she developed new recipes to utilize them.

The three of them have accustomed Cincinnati to Nouvelle Cuisine, wild game (every November), Cajun food (Jerry studied with Paul Prudhomme), free-range chicken, and seafood flown in daily from New Orleans.

Current favorites include mushrooms stuffed with redfish and wild rice, catfish in blue cornmeal, veal tenderloin with artichoke and mushrooms, and grilled free-range chicken with tasso Hollandaise, but there's always something new on the blackboard. Desserts change, too (try fresh peach mousse in

179

a cookie cup, if you're there in season), but you can count on their signature black bottom pie, and Grand Marnier cheese-cake.

"The dining public is really sophisticated," Howard said. "About half the people who come in here could prepare the same thing at home."

Perhaps. But at the Heritage, somehow it just tastes better.

The Heritage, 7664 Wooster Pike, Cincinnati, Ohio 45227, is open for lunch 11 a.m. to 3 p.m., Monday through Friday, for dinner 5:30 to 10 p.m. Monday through Thursday, until 11 p.m. Friday and Saturday. It is open on Sunday only for Mother's Day and Easter. (513)561-9300. Attire is "dressy casual;" jackets are preferred for men. All legal beverages are served, and there is an extensive wine list. Reservations are appreciated. AE, DC, MC, V. ($$$)

HERITAGE GRILLED SHRIMP

½ cup olive oil
2 cloves garlic, minced
2 teaspoons salt
1 Tablespoon chopped basil OR
l teaspoon dried basil
1 Tablespoon crushed red pepper

2 teaspoons dried Italian herbs
3 Tablespoons chopped parsley
1 ½ pounds raw shrimp, tail on

Combine first 8 ingredients, pour over shrimp in a bowl, and stir until shrimp is well coated. Cover tightly with plastic wrap, and marinate 4 to 6 hours or overnight. Remove shrimp from marinade and grill over charcoal or broil for 2 minutes on each side, or until done. Serves 6 as appetizer, 4 as main course.

HERITAGE POACHED BREAST OF CHICKEN WITH LEMON THYME BUERRE BLANC

7 cups chicken stock, divided
Eight 7- or 8-ounce boneless, skinless chicken breasts

3 Tablespoons basil, chopped
1 ½ Tablespoons chives, snipped
1 teaspoon garlic, minced

180

1 Tablespoon shallots, minced
3 Tablespoons lemon thyme
2 Tablespoons green peppercorns
1 cup red wine vinegar
8 ounces butter, in ½-inch pieces
Chive flowers and lemon thyme flowers for garnish

In saucepan, bring 4 cups stock to boil, add chicken breasts, and poach for 10 to 12 minutes. In another pan, combine 3 cups stock with herbs and spices and simmer until volume is reduced to 1 cup. Add red wine vinegar, simmer 2 minutes, then whip butter into sauce until well blended. Pour sauce over drained chicken, and garnish with chive and thyme flowers. Serves 8.

HERITAGE PASTA SALAD WITH HERB VINAIGRETTE

Herb vinaigrette (see below)
½ pound cooked, cooled pasta
1 ½ cups sliced mushrooms
1 cup sliced scallion tops
1 cup chopped tomatoes
2 cups turkey, ham, or chicken, in julienne
2 cups broccoli florets, slightly cooked
Parmesan cheese

Toss pasta and vegetables with herb vinaigrette, and add Parmesan cheese to taste. Serves 8 to 10.

For herb vinaigrette:
⅔ cup wine vinegar
2 or 3 cloves garlic, crushed
2 Tablespoons Dijon mustard
2 teaspoons cracked black pepper
¼ cup Parmesan cheese
1 cup chopped basil leaves
⅔ cup olive oil
⅔ cup salad oil
Salt to taste

In bowl, combine vinegar, garlic, mustard, pepper, Parmesan cheese, and basil. Set aside 30 minutes to blend flavors. Add oils to vinegar mixture and blend well. Yields about 2 ½ cups.

THE ROOKWOOD POTTERY
Cincinnati

Nicholas Longworth arrived in Cincinnati early in the nineteenth century, and set about founding one of the city's earliest and most stable fortunes. A successful lawyer, he gave up that practice to devote his time to his real estate holdings, which included vineyards on the slopes of a hill overlooking the city. Land he donated here became the site of the Cincinnati Observatory in 1843; President John Quincy Adams came for the dedication, and Mount Adams was named in his honor.

Longworth's granddaughter, Maria Longworth Nichols (later Storer) began a pottery in an old schoolhouse in 1880, contributing to a widespread interest in art pottery. Many well-to-do women were studying under- and over-glaze painting as an art form, and as a gainful employment for women; by 1891, ten thousand women in the United States were working in ceramics, and half of them earned their living by this means.

Mrs. Nichols named her pottery "Rookwood," for the word's similarity to Wedgwood, and for her father's summer home. The first kiln was drawn on Thanksgiving Day, 1880, and in the Paris Exposition of 1900, Rookwood Pottery was numbered among the five best in the world.

In 1891, a spacious new pottery was built on Mount Adams. In the Tudor Revival style, it had dark, exposed timbers, light stucco walls, leaded and stained glass windows, and a multi-gabled roof. Massive kilns burned oil, and the basement was used for clay storage and preparation. The pottery ceased business in 1967, and the building was placed on the National Register in 1972.

The portion now used as a restaurant has been skillfully adapted for the purpose; large open areas are decorated with photographs of the pottery in its heyday, and there is a showcase of magnificent examples of Rookwood Pottery at one end of the dining room. Intimate dining areas inside the old kilns are fun, and guests are free to wander about and examine the unusual old building.

Rookwood Pottery promises— and delivers— some of the best hamburgers you're likely to find. Half a pound of beef may be garnished with many toppings and colorful names:

Erkenbrecherburgher has bacon and Cheddar cheese; Blackenedburgher follows the current Cajun craze.

Soups and appetizers are good starters for a hearty meal at Rookwood Pottery, or are able to stand on their own, perhaps with a generous salad, topped with homemade dressings. A good one to try is the Popeye Salad, with spinach, mushrooms, black olives, cherry tomatoes, and cucumbers.

Chef Patrick Staples is gradually incorporating more regional foods and homemade pastas into the menu. However tempting they may be, leave room for Strawberries Bourbonnaise, with a caramel/bourbon sauce, or a sundae you make yourself, with four ice creams every day and lots of toppings.

Rookwood Pottery, 1077 Celestial Street, Cincinnati 45202, is open 7 days a week, with continuous service. Sunday through Thursday, hours are 11:30 a.m. to 10 p.m.; Friday and Saturday until 1 a.m. (513)721-5456. Dress is casual (shirts and shoes required), and all legal beverages are served, including Sunday. Reservations are accepted only for parties of 15 or more. Children's menu is available. AE, CB, DC, MC, V. ($$)

ROOKWOOD POTTERY CAJUN SHRIMP SCAMPI

5 or 6 medium shrimp
1 ½ ounces mushrooms, diced
3 ounces tomatoes, diced
1 ½ ounces scallions, diced
Butter for sautéeing
3 ounces white wine
1 teaspoon Cajun seasoning
Softened butter
Flour
4 ounces hot, cooked, linguine noodles

In large skillet, sauté shrimp, mushrooms, tomatoes, and scallions. Add wine and seasoning. Simmer, and stir in bits of a paste made of butter and flour to thicken to proper consistency. Serve over hot noodles. One serving.

ROOKWOOD POTTERY CRAB AND SHRIMP FETTUCINE

5 medium shrimp
2 ounces crabmeat
3 ounces tomatoes, diced
1 ½ ounces mushrooms, diced
4 ½ ounces hot, cooked spinach noodles
Butter for sautéeing
5 ounces shrimp and crab sauce (see note)

In large skillet, sauté shrimp, crabmeat, tomatoes, mushrooms, and noodles in butter until done; add sauce and heat through. One serving.

Note: Chef Staples makes this in large quantities. A good substitute may be made of 1 Tablespoon butter, 1 Tablespoon flour, and 5 ounces hot milk cooked together over medium heat until thickened, then seasoned to taste with shrimp and crabmeat.

ROOKWOOD POTTERY PASTA ALLA ROMA

4 ounces spinach noodles
1 ½ ounces mushrooms, diced
2 ounces diced tomatoes
2 ounces cauliflower florets
2 ounces broccoli florets
3 ounces ham, diced
¾ teaspoon minced garlic
Butter for sautéeing
4 ounces tomato sauce
1 ounce heavy cream
Parmesan cheese for topping

In large skillet, sauté noodles, mushrooms, tomatoes, cauliflower, broccoli, ham, and garlic. Blend in tomato sauce and cream. Place on ovenproof serving dish, top with Parmesan cheese, and run under broiler to brown. One serving.

ARNOLD'S BAR AND GRILL
Cincinnati

Known as "Queen City of the West" from early in its history, Cincinnati attracted settlers from many cultures and all walks of life. In 1842, Charles Dickens, who found little to like in America, called it "A beautiful city, cheerful, thriving, animated."

Bustling, brawling, mid-nineteenth-century Cincinnati was the world's greatest pork-packing center, nicknamed "Porkopolis"; related products of lard, oil, soap, and candles were also produced in large quantities.

Other industries made fabrics and clothing, iron, leather goods, steam engines, furniture, beer and wine. In 1858, the University of Cincinnati opened, followed by the Cincinnati Symphony Orchestra and the Cincinnati Conservatory of Music. Then, as now, manufacturing and society, high and low culture, rubbed shoulders happily, in one of the country's most diversified cities.

In 1861, Amos Arnold opened a tavern in half an Eighth street building, sharing space with a tannery and feed store that he later took over for a "Ladies' Sitting Room." Living on the third floor, the Arnold family used a separate entrance, and had a small garden in the rear. Additional dining rooms and rooms for boarders occupied the second floor. Amos was succeeded in the 1890s by Hugo, who was followed by his son Elmer in the 1920s.

Near the courthouse and office buildings, early Arnold's relied on businessmen's lunch, closing early in the evening, although a bricked-up basement tunnel and a bathtub on the second floor lend credence to rumors that illegal beverages were provided during prohibition.

James R. (Jim) Tarbell, proprietor since 1976, ably assisted by manager Shirley Cunningham, maintains Arnold's atmosphere. "It's very real," he said, "for the most part, the way it was in 1861."

Lawyers, artists, workmen, business people, musicians, librarians, and university personnel— the diverse population that has made the city a success— rub elbows at Arnold's, often sharing tables and enjoying each other as well as the food.

At lunch, hearty salads, sandwiches and pastas are popular,

with a daily special menu of casseroles and soups offering a wide choice. For dinner, try Nona Sauca, a baked garlic chicken with Italian sausage served over mostaciolli, or Arnold's famous Greek Spaghetti, with olives, green pepper, onion, bacon and mushrooms— and no tomatoes. All dishes are prepared from scratch and to order, with emphasis on fresh ingredients, and you can end with Mrs. Tarbell's homemade fruit pie or something rich and gooey from the day's specials.

The garden is open seasonally, and there's traditional music every night. Cincinnati's oldest continuously operating bar is everyone's favorite place.

Arnold's, 210 E. 8th, Cincinnati, Ohio 45202, is between Main and Sycamore, and is open Monday through Friday from 11 a.m. to 1 a.m., and from 4 p.m. to 1 a.m. Saturday, with continuous service; hot food is not served after 10 p.m. on weeknights. (513)421-6234. Dress is casual, "But not TOO casual," all legal beverages are served, and reservations are accepted for large groups only. Arnold's is usually closed for 2 weeks in August. No credit cards are accepted, although personal checks are. ($$)

ARNOLD'S BLACK BEAN SOUP

2 cups dry black beans
1 clove garlic, minced
1 onion, chopped
2 stalks celery, chopped
1 green pepper, chopped
Oil for sautéeing
1 ½ gallons water
⅛ cup sherry wine

½ teaspoon dry mustard
¼ teaspoon crushed red
  pepper
½ teaspoon salt
Lemon juice
Grated hard-cooked egg
  for garnish

Clean beans, cover with water and bring to boil. Remove from heat and cover for 1 hour. In large pot, sauté vegetables and spices in oil to cover bottom of pot. Add beans and water, and cook until beans are soft. Add sherry, mustard, salt and pepper, and simmer. Just before serving, add a couple of squeezes of lemon. Yields about a gallon.

ARNOLD'S SEAFOOD PASTA

3 ounces garlic butter (see below)

6 ounces raw seafood (cod, halibut, shrimp, scallops, and salmon)

¼ red sweet pepper, cut in strips

½ small zucchini, cut in thin half-rounds

3 water chestnuts, sliced

Hot, cooked linguini

In skillet, heat garlic butter and sauté seafood and vegetables, covered, over low heat until fish is done, about 6 minutes. Serve over linguini. One serving.

For garlic butter: In skillet, sauté 3 cloves garlic, chopped, in ⅓ cup butter over low heat about 5 minutes. Remove from heat, and add ⅓ cup olive oil and ¼ cup vegetable oil. Yields enough to make 6 or 8 servings of seafood pasta.

ARNOLD'S FARM HOUSE PIE

One 9-inch baked pie shell

3 ounces grated Swiss cheese

3 ounces crumbled cooked bacon

½ bunch broccoli, steamed and chopped

6 or 8 ounces shredded, cooked chicken

2 eggs

2 ¼ cups milk

1 ½ Tablespoons flour

⅛ teaspoon salt

Pinch of nutmeg

Layer cheese, bacon, broccoli, and chicken in pie shell. In large bowl, beat remaining ingredients together well, and pour over vegetables. Bake 1 hour at 350 degrees. Serves 5.

GRAMMER'S
Cincinnati

So many Germans settled in nineteenth-century Cincinnati that a German community of some 10,000 people developed out Vine Street, across the canal. In the German tradition, the area had an average beer consumption of thirty gallons per person per year, more than any city in the country.

"Over the Rhine" was very European, with beer gardens and singing halls, quaint red brick houses with scrubbed stone steps, German services in the churches, and German newspapers. Restaurants, bakeries, and groceries had German signs, and German was heard on the streets more often than English.

Anton Grammer, an Over the Rhine baker, built a restaurant across the street from his bakery in 1872. When he died in 1911, his son, Frank, demolished the adjacent 1830s Lutheran church, leaving its three-foot thick stone foundation, and built a new restaurant, importing a magnificent beveled and leaded glass storefront from Germany. Frank, a bachelor, lived upstairs, and operated the restaurant until his death in 1950.

By that time, most of the Germans had left Over the Rhine, and the neighborhood had deteriorated, although Grammer's remained a popular restaurant, with a menu of German foods.

When James R. ('Jim') Tarbell, known for his restoration of Arnold's Bar and Grill, became proprietor of Grammer's in 1984, it was his aim to return it to its days of glory. The handsome mahogany and stained glass bar and 1940s murals have been restored; bricked-up windows have been opened, and restoration of the building— and the menu— continues. Tarbell and manager Bill Cunningham have kept the German flavors, but have lightened the food for modern tastes.

There's a vegetarian vegetable soup, for instance, and a Veal and Onion Tart with raisins in a flaky pastry. Luncheon choices include the Fleisch Teller (meat plate) of liverwurst, beef tongue, mettwurst, and cheeses on a bed of lettuce with potato salad, and sandwiches such as Holsteiner sausage on pumpernickel, with a dark beer Cheddar cheese sauce. At dinner, Sauerbraten with Potato Pancake shares billing with Grilled Sirloin with Zinfandel sauce. Side orders of Real Mashed Potatoes and Braised Red Cabbage with Apples are honest and delicious, as are fresh fruit strudels and Black Forest cake for dessert.

Grammer's Restaurant, 1440 Walnut Street, Cincinnati 45210, is at the corner of Liberty Street, where there is a large, walled parking area. It is open 11 a.m. to 11 p.m., Monday through Thursday, to 1 a.m. Friday and Saturday, with continuous service, although all items are not available mid-afternoon. (513) 721-6570. Dress is casual, but "Not TOO casual," all legal beverages are served, and reservations are accepted, required for parties of 6 or more. AE, DC, MC, V. ($$)

GRAMMER'S SAUERKRAUT BALLS

1 pound dry, seasoned mashed potatoes
1 ½ pounds sauerkraut, squeezed dry
4 ounces chopped ham
1 Tablespoon chopped parsley
2 Tablespoons chopped scallions
1 Tablespoon mustard
Salt and pepper
Flour for breading
1 egg, beaten with 2 Tablespoons water
Fine bread crumbs for breading
Oil for frying

Combine first 7 ingredients thoroughly. Roll into 1-inch balls, then roll balls in flour, egg wash, and bread crumbs. Deep fry or pan fry golden brown. Yields about 2 ½ dozen.

GRAMMER'S THREE CHEESE AND HERB STRUDEL

½ pound Feta cheese
¼ pound cream cheese
¼ pound cottage cheese
⅛ teaspoon garlic powder
⅛ teaspoon black pepper
½ teaspoon dill seed
1 Tablespoon chopped parsley
1 Tablespoon chopped scallions
10 sheets phyllo (filo) pastry
CLARIFIED butter
Sesame seeds

In large bowl, thoroughly mix first 8 ingredients. Brush each sheet of pastry with CLARIFIED butter; place 2 sheets together to make five double layers. With knife, cut sheets in half lengthwise. Divide cheese mixture into 10 portions, and spread one portion of cheese down center of each strip of pastry. Turn long edges of pastry toward center, and roll up short edges, as an egg roll. Brush strudels with butter and sprinkle with sesame seeds. Place on buttered sheet pan and bake at 400 degrees for 12 to 15 minutes, or until crisp. Serves 5.

GRAMMER'S CHICKEN PAPRIKASH

5 chicken breasts, boned
Marjoram
Sage
Thyme
White wine
Vegetable oil
Sweet Hungarian paprika

8 ounces bacon, diced
5 ounces onion, chopped
½ pound mushrooms,
    quartered
½ cup flour
1 ½ cups chicken stock
Salt and pepper

Place chicken flesh side up on a tray, sprinkle with a pinch each of marjoram, sage, thyme, a little white wine, and oil. Cover with paprika and marinate 2 to 3 hours.

In braising pan, fry bacon crisp, add onion, and cook until clear. Add mushrooms, flour, and 2 Tablespoons paprika, and cook, stirring continuously, to a paste. Slowly add stock, 1 ounce white wine, additional herbs, and garlic. Simmer until sauce is desired consistency. Season. Chicken may be broiled or sautéed in butter, adding sauce when served, or it may be simmered in the sauce until done. Serves 5.

THE IRON HORSE INN
Glendale

When the Cincinnati, Hamilton, and Dayton railroad was under construction in the 1840s, a labor camp was set up along the right-of-way. After it was dismantled, and just before the first train ran in 1851, what is believed to be the first planned subdivision village in America was platted along the tracks.

Intended for railroad officials and business executives, Glendale's lots were from one to twenty acres, on forested, rolling hills. Streets curved, following the terrain, and substantial houses were expected, and were built, starting in 1852, resulting in a charming village of several mid-19th-century architectural styles. The Glendale Historic District was placed on the National Register in 1976; a National Landmark, it was the first historic district in Ohio so designated.

On Glendale's Village Square, shops and a depot were built in 1880 to replace earlier structures destroyed by fire. Additional shops, police station, and city offices cluster around the depot, once the center of Glendale's activity.

Bracker (pronounced BRAKE er) Tavern, on one side of the square, was, according to tradition, a drover's tavern, frequented by those who escorted herds of cattle along the path (now the railroad) to the stockyards, possibly as early as 1839, and certainly before 1856.

A handsome, square, two-story brick building, altered over the years, it has retained its bracketed gable/hip roof and probably the original upstairs windows, as well as interior molding and the stairwell. As the Iron Horse Inn, it continues a long tradition of serving food and drink to its patrons.

There is a comfortable men's-club atmosphere at the Iron Horse, which takes its logo from the 1856 steam engine shown in an early photograph of the train station. The bar, relocated, remains from the tavern's days as an ice-cream parlor, as do the barstools. Photographs and artifacts from Glendale's past carry out a subdued railroad motif, complimenting the brown, black, and butterscotch decor in the two downstairs dining rooms.

Owner Dewey Huff is the first Glendale native to own the restaurant, and, with Chef Robert Shields, has brought it to new culinary heights. Everything here is made from scratch—

even potato chips— and stocks are simmered for eighteen hours. There's a different soup every day, plus the Glendale Clam Chowder, and fresh seafoods and steaks are cut on the premises. Chef Shields makes seafoods a specialty.

"I enjoy working with seafood," he said. "I think anyone can cook prime rib."

He does that, too, of course, and very well. Other specialties are roast duckling with orange sauce, chicken breast with chicken mousse and julienne vegetables, and veal medallions with Chanterelle mushrooms and artichoke bottoms.

Lighter entrées join sandwiches and hearty salads at luncheon; Almond Chicken Salad in half a pineapple with fruit, and Gulf Combo Salad with shrimp, scallops, and crab are good summer choices.

At any meal, desserts are outstanding, and the Bavarian Mud Pie, a mocha Bavarian cream in a cookie crust, topped with chocolate fudge and whipped cream, is a memorable eating experience.

The Iron Horse Inn, 40 Village Square, Glendale, Ohio 45246, is open for lunch 11:30 a.m. to 2:30 p.m. Monday through Saturday, for dinner 5:30 to 9:30 p.m. Monday through Thursday, to 11 p.m. Friday and Saturday. (513)771-2050. Most men wear ties, all legal beverages are available, and reservations are suggested, preferred for groups of 6 or more. Especially busy times are during "Glendale Holiday House Tour," second weekend in December, and the street fair, second Saturday in September. AE, DC. MC, V. ($$$)

IRON HORSE INN LOBSTER BISQUE

4 medium lobster bodies
1 yellow onion, quartered
1 bunch celery tops and leaves
4 whole bay leaves
1 teaspoon rosemary
1 teaspoon thyme
1 ½ gallons Glendale Spring water (or substitute)

1 cup tomato puree
2 cups heavy cream
½ cup CLARIFIED butter
1 ½ cups flour
½ cup dry sherry wine

In large oven-proof pot, roast lobster bodies at 375 degrees for 30 minutes. Remove from oven and place over burner. Add onion, celery, bay leaves, herbs, and water. Bring to boil, reduce heat, and simmer 45 minutes. Lift out lobster bodies and discard. Whisk in tomato purée and cream. Blend CLARIFIED butter and flour to a paste; pinch bits of this off and whisk into soup to thicken to consistency of a creamy salad dressing. Add sherry just before serving. Strain through fine cheese cloth. Serves 8.

IRON HORSE INN SMOKED SALMON FETTUCCINE

½ cup white wine
4 cups pre-cooked
  fettuccine noodles
20 fresh asparagus tips
¼ cup freshly grated
  Parmesan cheese

¾ cup heavy cream
½ pound smoked salmon,
  cubed
1 teaspoon capers
Additional Parmesan
  cheese

In a 2-quart skillet over medium heat, place wine, noodles, asparagus, cheese, and cream. Bring to a boil, then reduce heat to simmer. Add salmon and capers just long enough for salmon to be slightly broken. Portion onto 4 dinner plates and sprinkle with Parmesan cheese. Serves 4.

GRAND FINALE
Glendale

On the southeast corner of Sharon Road and Congress Avenue, just inside the historic area of Glendale, a two-story commercial building was erected about 1875. It is believed to have been included with the house across the street at a sheriff's sale of the property of John Corcoran, in December, 1911.

The new owner, John J. Kelley, was a saloon keeper; a picture exists of a horsedrawn Wiedemann beer wagon in front of the tavern. A grocery was added in the back, and the bar vanished during prohibition. "Kelley's Market," in the care of two elderly sisters who lived upstairs, continued in operation until the late 1960's. With canned goods still on the shelves, the store remained closed until it was discovered by Cindy and Larry Youse, who turned it into a restaurant.

"It was love at first sight," Cindy said, "but it was just a mess. It looked like it was waiting for the wrecker's ball."

"It had been abandoned for five years," Larry added. "The ladies had died and left all the food in the store."

The Youses cleaned and restored the building, decorating the downstairs rooms with oak tables and chairs and lots of plants, filling "The Attic" bar with toys, and building a courtyard for outdoor dining. Grand Finale opened in August, 1975.

The name was chosen because the restaurant was intended as a showcase for Larry's superb desserts; crêpes and quiches were added, and they have now "evolved to serving just about everything," Larry said.

Terming their output "Creative American Cuisine," they make their own Italian sausage, bakers come in nightly to start the excellent homemade breads, and an effort is made to offer new and adventurous items. "When we opened up," Cindy said, "no one in Ohio had ever heard of crêpes. We're constantly trying to introduce unfamiliar things."

Daily blackboard listings of three appetizer and three entrée specials, soup du jour, and frequent dessert specials add to an extensive menu. Fresh mushrooms baked in cheese, an appetizer; Savannah Salad of shrimp, scallops, crabmeat, and greens; and Creole Crêpes are typical of the offerings on all menus. Light luncheon specialties and heartier dinner ones are added. Sunday brunch buffet is all you can eat of everyone's favorites, including hot biscuits, fried chicken livers, home-made bread pudding, and samples of quiches, crêpes, and desserts.

Grand Finale desserts could be a meal— and doubtless have been, for some— due to their spectacular size and irresistible content. Sky-high mousse pies, chocolate in a pecan crust, or lime with hazelnut, are house signatures. At dinner, add flaming crêpes, Cherries Jubilee, and Apple Cobbler Flambé.

Grand Finale, Sharon Road at Congress Avenue, Glendale, Ohio 45246, is open Tuesday through Saturday from 11:30 a.m. to 11 p.m., with continuous service. Sunday brunch buffet is 10:30 to 3 p.m.; dinner is 5 to 10 p.m. (513)771-5923. Attire is casual to dressy, all legal beverages are served, including Sunday, and weeknight reservations are recommended; reservations are not accepted for Saturday night or Sunday brunch. AE, CB, DC MC, V. ($$)

GRAND FINALE STEAK SALAD ANNIE

One 6-ounce filet mignon, trimmed
6 ounces your favorite vinaigrette dressing
3 garlic cloves, finely diced
3 shakes hot sauce
3 cups mixed salad greens
4 ounces mushrooms, sliced thin
4 ounces Swiss cheese, in 1-inch squares
12 medium gulf shrimp, cooked and chilled
4 strips bacon, cooked crisp, then crumbled
1 scallion, finely chopped
½ tablespoon chopped parsley

Char-grill filet medium rare. Slice very thin, in bite-sized pieces, and marinate in mixture of dressing, garlic, and hot sauce for 30 minutes in the freezer, stirring occasionally. In chilled serving bowl, arrange lettuce, top with mushrooms and cheese, circle with shrimp, then arrange filet in center. Sprinkle with bacon, onions, and parsley. Use reserved marinade to dress salad. Serves 1 or 2 as entrée, 4 as salad.

GRAND FINALE BROCHETTE JAMBALAYA

6 or 8 chunks pre-cooked
  ham
Four ½-inch slices
  zucchini
6 jumbo green shrimp

2 small cloves garlic,
  mashed
½ cup butter
½ cup raw bay scallops
Melted margarine

Thread ham, zucchini, and shrimp on two skewers. In saucepan, heat garlic in butter and pour over scallops in a ramekin. Place skewers and ramekin on a cookie sheet, and drizzle skewers with margarine. Bake 10 to 15 minutes at 315 degrees, until seafood is firm and ham is hot through. Serve with hot drawn butter and lemon wedges. One serving.

THE GRAND FINALE GRAND TRIFLE

4 cups pound or yellow
  cake chunks
1 cup fresh or frozen,
  thawed strawberries in
  syrup
4 ounces port wine
4 ounces cream sherry
8 large scoops rich vanilla
  ice cream or custard
1 cup fresh or frozen,
  thawed raspberries in
  syrup

1 ½ to 2 cups heavy cream,
  whipped
¼ cup toasted slivered
  almonds
8 maraschino or chocolate
  covered cherries for
  garnish

In 8 large brandy snifters or a 2-quart clear glass bowl, layer ingredients in order given and garnish with cherries. Chill about an hour to blend flavors. Serves 8.

INDEX TO RESTAURANTS

INDEX TO RECIPES